moshi monsters™

CHARACTER ENCYCLOPEDIA

Written by Steve Cleverley,
Lauren Holowaty, and Claire Sipi

CONTENTS

INTRODUCTION

Welcome to the gloopendous world of Moshi Monsters, a weird and wonderful place brimming with crazy critters of all shapes and sizes. These pages are crammed with all kinds of clawsome characters, from wacky Moshi shopkeepers and ghostly pirates to cute Moshlings, cosmic Zoshlings, and diabolical baddies. You'll even find some genuine gooperstars and Roarkers, too (they're workers in case you're wondering). Moshi-tastic!

Monsters

Lots of monsters live in Monstro City, but the most common types are the flutterly amazing Luvli, very furry Furi, choptastic Katsuma, smokin' Diavlo, huggalicious Poppet, and rockin' Zommer.

Moshlings

Monsters love collecting these teeny weeny critters as pets. There are loads of different types of Moshlings, such as cuddly Fluffies, tasty Foodies, and not-so-spooky Spookies. Each type has several species, so if you catch a Fluffie it could be a Dinky Dreamcloud, Pluff, Funny Bunny, or Pixel-Munching Snaffler!

4

C.L.O.N.C.

C.L.O.N.C. (the Criminal League of Naughty Critters) has many mysterious members, including the dastardly Dr. Strangeglove. Along with his cohorts in crime, this twisted Glumper extraordinaire plans to bring Monstro City to its knees. Mwah-ha-ha-haaa!

Glumps

These are Dr. Strangeglove's horrible minions. They were once cute, innocent Moshlings, but they have been put through his ghastly Glumping Machine, turning them into an army of dimwitted goons sent out to cause mischief.

Super Moshis

Led by Elder Furi, a team of the bravest, most elite monsters has come together to put an end to C.L.O.N.C.'s evil deeds.

AGONY ANT

Got a monster problem? Need some goopendous advice? Then talk to Agony Ant. She may be one of Monstro City's smallest residents, but she has some BIG advice. Agony Ant has a regular column in *The Daily Growl*, in which she passes on her wisdom to any troubled monster readers.

Mystical mission
Agony doesn't think of her job as work—she loves sharing her monsterific psychic predictions with her furry readers.

Agony's antennae start to quiver when she has a "psychic" feeling.

Funky green glasses help Agony gaze into her crystal ball.

DATA FILE
Hangout: *The Daily Growl* office
Job: Psychic fortune teller
Newspaper chums: Roary Scrawl, Ruby Scribblez

Teen Agony
As a young Ant, Agony used to hang out in Hokery Pokery Heights. It was there that she met a gaggle of Woolly Blue Hoodoos and some Furry Heebees. These wise old Moshlings taught her everything they knew about fortune telling and mysticism—and Agony Ant found her calling!

The "mystic" look is completed with a flowing robe and crystal necklace.

ANGEL

The SkyPony

DATA FILE

Moshling type: Ponies
Species: SkyPony
Habitat: Cloud 9 above Blocky Mountains
Ponie pals: Gigi, Mr. Snoodle, Priscilla

Until recently, these supremely secretive creatures were thought to exist only in fairy tales. At bedtime, young monsters were told legends of the SkyPonies' deeds. Then one day, *The Daily Growl* reported that a herd of SkyPonies had appeared, as if by magic, on a pink cloud, high above Mount Sillimanjaro.

The true powers of the SkyPonies' magical horns are shrouded in secrecy.

Timid trotters

These shy little ponies rarely leave the safety of the clouds to visit ground level. If you are lucky enough to meet one, they will tell you tales of a strange world in the sky where everything is wonderfully soft and fluffy.

Heavenly harps

SkyPonies fly in the skies around Cloud 9. If you listen carefully, you might hear them playing their heavenly harp music, occasionally interrupted by loud slurping noises as they guzzle maple syrup!

Long, dainty legs and soft hooves are ideal for cloud hopping.

Feathery tails and wings help SkyPonies float and fly gracefully.

7

ART LEE

Do you know your Da Pinchis from your Warthols? Well, if art is your thang, make a trip to see Art Lee in one of the coolest hangouts in town (literally—the hairier you are, the warmer you'll be!). Pop down to the Underground Tunnels and you'll find Monstro City's hottest and most exciting new pop artist!

Moaning LEEsa

Art can paint his "Smiling Face" in no time. He may be underground at the moment, but next year his own "Moaning LEEsa" could be hanging in the Googenheim!

DATA FILE

Hangout: The Underground Tunnels

Job: Amateur graffiti artist

Ambition: To be the next Danksy

Stylin' mushroom cap is Monstro City's answer to the beret.

Large paintbrush (key tool of the trade)

Amateur artist

He may be new to painting, but Art Lee knows how to create some super-sweet works of pop art. With his pots of paint and splat-tastic brushes, this talented little monster brightens up those gloomy tunnel walls with his monstrous creations!

As all artists know, sticking your tongue out helps the creative juices flow!

8

BABS

Babs' Boutique Shop Owner

DATA FILE

Hangout: The Port

Job: Shopkeeper and owner of Babs' Boutique

Likes: Perfect hair, using Sneeze Wax

If it is the extraordinary and the rare you are looking for, stroll on down to The Port. The boutique-alicious Babs has a fangtastic shop full of stuff that you can't lay your furry paws on anywhere else in the City. If you'd like a spotlit floor fit for a monSTAR or a door from a space rocket, Babs' Boutique is the place to go.

Funky bandana holds hair in place.

Babs' crowning glory is her perfectly styled hair.

Boutique babe

Babs was the first merchant to open her doors at The Port. Always welcoming with her monstrous smile, Babs has sold thousands of unusual items to her hairy customers.

Get the look! Stripes are moshi-tabulous in Monstro City, darling.

Hairy locks

Those sprouting spikes don't just happen! If you want a beautiful hairy-style like Babs, pop into her Boutique and she'll sell you a jar of the Sneeze Wax Company's floor wax. Just rub the icky wax through your hair—Babs swears it contains the perfect conditioning properties!

Lazy Beach Dude

BA BARNACL-

Baz Barnacle is a big beach bum! Every day he hangs out at Bleurgh Beach, surfing the waves and toasting his huge hairy body on the sand. Give him a bucketful of sand to guzzle and a bowl of sea water, and Baz is in monster bliss. All that lazing in the sun has made him a bit fried!

DATA FILE

Location: Bleurgh Beach

Job: Running a surf shop

Best bud: Bonzer the Prawn

Likes: Silly sandy snacks, beach-partying the night away

Once bright green, Baz's hat has faded in the sun.

Surf shack

Baz has a rickety old surf shack where he sells oddities like shark-bitten surfboards. Most of his goods were borrowed (or swiped!) from his salty seadog cousin, Captain Buck the pirate.

Baz's shaggy monster beard is always full of sand.

BBQ beast

Baz rarely visits the City. For starters, that would require a monster effort to shift his furry bulk off the sand. And anyway, he would rather be down at the beach day and night, partying with his best friend, Bonzer the Prawn. Time to throw another sandcastle on the barbecue!

Baz works the beach look with flip-flops and a garish shirt.

10

BEAU SQUIDDLY

DATA FILE

Location: The Port

Job: Fisherman and ex-jazz musician

Likes: Fishing to feed his caviar obsession, reminiscing

Monstro City proudly presents... Beau Squiddly! This musical maestro was once a jazz gooperstar who was a *Daily Growl* Top 10 best new artist. Sadly, Beau's career plummeted and he blew his fortune. These days he works long hours as a fisherman to scrape together just enough Rox to feed his monstrous caviar habit.

Beau's hat is all that remains from his jazz days.

Beau keeps a jar of caviar under his hat.

Beau's mouth is gloomy and downcast when he thinks about the past.

Fame is a fickle friend

Unfortunately for Squiddly, celebrity life went straight to his furry head. A few chart-topping hits and several platinum albums later, Beau had splurged his riches on a fine dining addiction and too many trips to Horrods and Tyra's Spa.

Beau-tastic!

Doo-wop, de-dum, diddly-squiddly, shoowop-di-doo! Beau will never forget his glory days as a jazz legend. Better get singing for your supper then, Squiddly!

11

BENTLEY

Supah Loofahs like Bentley may be tiny, but they can soak up half an ocean's worth of water! Never drop one in Potion Ocean or there will be a Fishie mutiny on your hands! Posh Moshi monsters used to use Supah Loofahs to clean their hairy backs, but these spongy critters are much happier soaking up water than they are scrubbing.

Shower power
Supah Loofahs love spending hours soaking under a steaming hot power shower—as long as there isn't a bottle of shower gel in sight. They hate getting the bubbles in their eyes!

DATA FILE
Moshling type: Undiscovered
Species: Supah Loofah
Habitat: Reggae Reef
Often spotted:
In bathrooms
across Monstro City

Loofahs hate flaky skin, so they keep their spongy bodies nice and moist.

Lounging Loofahs
You'll find Bentley and the other Supah Loofahs chillin' out at Reggae Reef, soaking up the water and cool vibes. The spongy Moshlings always sit in the shade though, as the sun causes them to dry up and crumble into lots of pieces. Disaster!

Supah Loofahs are so chilled out, they can hardly be bothered to move!

12

BERT

Gift Island Roarker

DATA FILE

Location: Gift Island

Job: Sorting and shoveling gifts

Often spotted: Staring out at sea

Bert works hard on Gift Island, checking off lists of presents, sorting them, and shoveling the gifts into piles for delivery. Not much else is known about this shy little critter as he tends to avoid other monsters. Bashful Bert rarely chats with his co-workers—he likes to stay completely focused on the job.

Bert always wears his Gift Island Roarker's hat.

Monstrously shy
When you're as shy as Bert, Gift Island is a great place to work. There are always mountains of packages to hide behind when everything gets too intense!

Shovel for shifting parcels into piles

Scaredy-critter
Bert is terrified of the stories his co-workers tell of a giant monster who lurks in the murky waters around Gift Island and feasts on Jelly Fuzzes. With his shovel shaking in his paws and his eyes scanning the horizon, Burt's fear of this beast causes him to ooze bucket-loads of sweat. Poor Bert!

BETTY

The **ear-splitting** operatic yodeling of the MooMoo can be heard across the land—from the freezing heights of Sillimanjaro to their home village of StrudelHofen and bustling Main Street. The noise that Betty the MooMoo makes is enough to crack the most goopendous bone china—and has even triggered an avalanche or two!

DATA FILE

Moshling type: Noisies
Species: Yodeling MooMoo
Habitat: Anywhere mountainous
Noisie pals: Cherry Bomb, Boomer, Judder

Pointy blue horns

Large ears for listening to own moo-sical singing

Operatic diva

Moshling MooMoos like Betty are opera-trained from an early age. They can sing for hours, only taking a break to scarf down schnitzel.

Miserable moo

Never tell a MooMoo a joke. When it comes to humor, these singing divas are monstrously lacking! Then again, if you had to listen to them for hours, you wouldn't be laughing either!

Dressed to perform in an opera costume

14

BIG BAD BILL

Woolly Blue Hoodoos like Big Bad Bill are ancient mystical creatures. These wise old furballs wander the wilderness looking for ingredients for their potions and monstrous new ideas. Although they are rarely spotted, you might just be able to tempt one out of the vegetation with a deep fried Oobla Doobla!

"Go do the Hoodoo!"

Woolly Blue Hoodoos rock! These hairy dudes have their own hit record—and Big Bad Bill has a starring role in the cool music video.

DATA FILE

Moshling type: Spookies
Species: Woolly Blue Hoodoo
Habitat: Gombala Gombala Jungle (according to legend)
Spookie chums: Ecto, Kissy, Squidge

Distinctive eye patch

A Hoodoo is never seen without a mystical Staff of Power.

Yellow tribal paint

Mystical monsters

Thorn in the paw, pain in the jaw? Hoodoos know everything there is to know about lotions, potions, hexes, and spells. They can cure all monstrous ailments with a bit of old flip-flop, a creepy crawly, and some mysterious chants.

Such long hair can cause itching, but a deep massage provides welcome relief.

15

He's big, he's blue, he's bad and he's got the most ridiculously small noggin—meet Big Chief Tiny Head! Once the proud owner of a huge head, this ludicrous C.L.O.N.C. agent now spends most of his time trying to find a way back to his former big-headed glory.

DATA FILE
Location: Currently unknown, somewhere in a teepee
Job: Member of C.L.O.N.C.
Likes: Hula dancing classes
Dislikes: Salad, forked tongues

Ornate feathered headdress hides TomaSquawk, Big Chief's vicious pet cuckoo.

Bongo Colada cocktail

Slurp!
This tropical terror waits in the jungle, hoping to grab Naughty Nutter coconut Moshlings so he can drink his favorite cocktail, Bongo Colada, from them.

Not so big head!
Big Chief was once wandering along in the Gombala Gombala Jungle, searching for some food. He came across a Woolly Blue Hoodoo frying some tasty Oobla Doobla. The greedy Chief tried to grab the Moshling's grub, but the angry Hoodoo put a hex on him that made his head shrink. Big Chief Tiny Head now bears a nasty grudge against all Hoodoos!

Big Chief wears gloopendously garish shirts and grass skirts!

BILLY BOB BAITMAN

Boot-a-licious!
Every time Billy Bob feels movement at the end of the line, he's excited that he might haul in a fish, but it's always the same green boot!

Day after day, Billy Bob Baitman's catch of the day is the same old boot! This unlucky fisherman sits on the pier at the end of Sludge Street, scanning the lake waters in vain. For poor Billy Bob, three eyes are definitely not better than one, but he is sure that he'll hook a fish one day. If nothing else he might get a different boot, so he'd have a matching pair!

Billy wears a baseball cap to keep the sun out of his three eyes when fishing.

Fishing rod made out of a long tree branch

DATA FILE
Location: Lake at the end of Sludge Street
Job: Fisherman
Ambition: To catch a fish!
Often spotted: Waiting in the same spot for hours

Beefy bait
Billy once decided to try a new tactic and use the meatball from his sandwich as bait. Unfortunately, Cali the Valley Mermaid swiped the meatball off his hook for dinner, leaving a very hungry fisherman! Poor Billy had to sit and smell the delicious scent of Cali's cooking wafting across the water!

Bright red bait on the end of Billy's line—but the fish don't seem to like it!

17

BJORN SQUISH

It's hard work being a Roarker... unless your name is Bjorn Squish, that is. Bjorn claims he does heavy construction work, all day, every day. But if you hang around Main Street, you'll soon see that the only hard work Bjorn does is lifting his sandwiches from his lunchbox into his mouth!

DATA FILE
Location: Main Street
Job: Roarker
Roarker co-workers: Ken Tickles, Rickety Boo
Dislikes: Crumbs in his bed

Orange hard hat to keep the Roarkers safe on site

Energy boost
Monstrous newsflash! Bjorn was actually seen working! He carried some boxes down at The Port, though it took him a week of extra-long lunch breaks to recover!

Handy log for sitting on—Bjorn needs a rest after all his (hard) work!

Bjorn makes the yummiest sandwiches in the whole City.

Scrumptious sandwiches!
Bjorn does make a gloopendous sandwich. When his supervisor, Dizzee Bolt, took a monster bite of his Green on Fly Bread, she drooled so much that she said he could eat sandwiches all day—as long as he brought in extras for the other Roarkers!

BLACK JACK

It was truly a dark day when evil villain Dr. Strangeglove's Glumping Machine spewed out the ball of badness that was to become Black Jack. Once a cute Moshling, this dangerous critter is now not only mean, but is the most ruthless Glump known to Glumpkind. Even the other Glumps quake at the sight of his ugly face!

Crashing cannonballs!

With his red eyes fuming and mouth drooling, Black Jack loves to shoot like a cannonball through the city streets, knocking monsters off their furry feet.

Crazy crook

Black Jack has learned well from his master, the elusive Dr. Strangeglove. On the Doctor's orders, he sneaks around Monstro City, scaring innocent Moshlings out of their hairy skins. The wicked Glump also disrupts the Super Moshis' heroic missions, by getting in their way and causing chaos!

Tuft of purple, spiky hair is good for poking victims.

Slimy gray and purple spots

DATA FILE
Location: Top Secret
Job: C.L.O.N.C. minion
Features: Threatening stare, spotty skin

Big clenched teeth are bared in menace.

19

BLINGO

Cruise on up to the Hipsta Hills near Ker-Ching Canyon if you want to hang out with the finest rhyming rappers, 'cause that's where the funky Flashy Foxes do their thing and show off some serious bling! Blingo's foxy crew are the leaders of the pack, sporting super-sharp shades and the slickest gear that Horrods has to offer.

Urban fox
Flashy Foxes dig breakdancing nearly as much as rapping. They never miss any opportunity to show off their cool moves on the streets of Monstro City.

The latest must-have cool cap

No monster has ever seen Blingo's eyes—he never takes off his shades!

DATA FILE:
Moshling type: Secrets
Species: Flashy Fox
Habitat: Hipsta Hills, overlooking Ker-Ching Canyon
Secret friend: Roxy

You've got to have some serious bling to be taken seriously as a Flashy Fox.

Rap monSTAR
Blingo took a break from smooth boom-box beats to record a slammin' solo rap on Zack Binspin's debut single. His singing was so fast that Zack didn't understand a word! Blingo's skills for lightning-quick rhymes are second-to-none, but he still recommends gargling with gooberry juice to avoid getting tongue-tied!

BLOOPY

What's blue, blobby, and badly behaved? Bloopy, of course! A mopey member of villainous Dr. Strangeglove's naughty gang of Glumps, Bloopy is always down in the dumps. Well, wouldn't you be monstrously depressed if your face looked like a squished blueberry?

Super Glump!
When Bloopy teamed up with the sickly criminal Sweet Tooth to cause monster mayhem, the Super Moshi heroes had to morph into a Bloopy look-alike to gain entry into the Candy Cane Caves. Yuck—not a good Super Moshi look!

Spiky purple clump of greasy Glump hair

DATA FILE
Location: Top Secret
Job: C.L.O.N.C. minion
Features:
Blue flabby skin, gloomy expression

Large pink miserable mouth is always moaning and groaning.

Blob of badness
It's hard to believe that Glumps started life as cute, cuddly little Moshlings, before the sinister Dr. Strangeglove got his hand(s) on them. Bloopy is a prime example. He loves to splat Moshlings with his Mega Glump Thumps—there is nothing cute about that!

21

BLURP

Blurp by name and batty by nature, the Batty Bubblefish is not the smartest Fishie in the school. Blurp and fellow bewildered Bubblefish spend most days swimming around trying to remember what they've done and where they've been. This makes them monstrously bad-tempered... well, for a few seconds anyway, until they forget what they're angry about!

Gloopendous!

Offer Blurp a fish stick at your own peril, 'cause you'll be in for a splat-tastic surprise. Batty Bubblefish hate fish fingers—and will splurt out gallons of icky gloop!

Spikes don't make this little Fishie the sharpest tool in the box.

Bulging eyes

Flippy, floppy fins for leaping and swimming in circles

Fishie fun

Bubblefish live in the fangtastically foamy waters beneath Fruit Falls. Go hang out at this Moshi paradise and you might see one of these puffed-up spikeballs cuddling an old flip-flop or blowing a gloopy raspberry. They are truly batty!

DATA FILE
Moshling type: Fishies
Species: Batty Bubblefish
Habitat: Fruit Falls
Fishie friends: Stanley, Fumble, Cali

BOBBI SINGSONG

DATA FILE
Moshling type: RoxStar
Species: Jollywood Singalong
Habitat: Jollywood
Celebrity pal: Zack Binspin

Coming soon to a town near you, singing sensation Bobbi SingSong! This big-haired, moustachioed gooperstar is taking Jollywood by storm with his melodious crooning and monsterific sitar playing. His hometown has paid him the highest honor by adopting his smash hit "Welcome to Jollywood" as its national anthem!

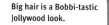
Big hair is a Bobbi-tastic Jollywood look.

Rickshaw rider!
Life in Jollywood is jolly good. Gooperstars cruise the hills in their limos. But Bobbi's no diva—he'd rather rattle around in his own rickshaw.

Moshi-tabulous moustache

Bobbi's sitar. Bobbi is the best sitar player in Jollywood, apart from his guru Pluckii StringSong.

Tranquil tune
Hyper-energetic Bobbi tries to relax before a gig by strumming on the strings of his sitar and meditating. Perhaps he should write the words to his mantra down, though, because he keeps forgetting them!

23

BONKERS

The rare critter Bonkers is probably the only one of his kind. When not chillin' and eating Pop Rox in his Sludgetown Apartment, he hangs out near the busy entrance to The Underground Disco. This crowd pleaser has learned to do tricks to entertain the Underground dwellers in order to earn enough Rox to pay his rent.

Jumping for joy!
Bonkers knows the more bonkers his tricks are, the more Rox the rich monstro-rati disco crowd will throw his way. His most bonkers to date is his spectacular double somersault backflip!

Big googly eyes give Bonkers his... well, bonkers look!

Long striped tail helps Bonkers launch himself for a backflip.

DATA FILE
Hangout: The Underground Tunnels

Job: Doing tricks to earn Rox for his rent

Likes: Jumping

Agent Bonkers
The rocks that Bonkers sits on in the Underground Tunnels hide a secret archway in the wall. Once, he used a magic trick to make the rocks disappear so the Super Moshis could use the opening to reach a hidden C.L.O.N.C. lab on one of their secret missions.

Springy legs and feet made for jumping!

BOOMER

Raaaargh! Quick, cover your ears—here come the Bigmouth Squiddly Dees from Eleventy Nook. Sweet-looking critters like Boomer are anything but cute. If one opens its gigantic purple-tongued mouth, run away because it's going to yell like a foghorn! And we're talking enough decibels to dislodge your earwax!

Big mouth!
Don't want your head blown off? Then DO NOT touch a Squiddly Dee. One tiny prod and the monstrous mouth will snap open with a S-H-R-I-E-K!

Soft, fluffy orange fur—but don't be fooled by its adorable appearance!

DATA FILE
Moshling type: Noisies
Species: Bigmouth Squiddly Dee
Habitat: Eleventy Nook
Noisie pals: Cherry Bomb, Judder, Betty

Layers and layers of soft toilet paper

Doctor's orders!
Boomer and the Squiddlies bandage their ears with toilet paper to protect them from their own shrieking. What a fangtastic idea! They often tuck some cough drops into the bandages, as their poor throats can get very sore and scratchy.

25

BRUISER

Bruiser, as his name suggests, is definitely the strongest and brawniest of evil Dr. Strangeglove's sinister squidgy sidekicks. This bruising, bullying Glump lives for a fight. If there's trouble to be found, you can be sure bloodthirsty Bruiser will sniff it out!

C.L.O.N.C. Clump

Bruiser was once ordered to check tickets at the entrance to villainous Sweet Tooth's circus. The Clump—or Glump in disguise—looked quite grotesque in his circus clown costume!

Angry-looking spots

Even Glumps need bandages on their cuts.

Bruiser's scarred skin makes for a scary sight!

War wounds

Bruiser collects scars like monsters collect Moshlings. He doesn't care that he looks like he's been dragged through the bushes backward—it just means that he can think of new names for his nasty fighting moves. His latest? "Scarface Smashes!"

DATA FILE

Location: Top Secret
Job: C.L.O.N.C. minion
Features: Big gap between his two front teeth, scars

BUBBA

DATA FILE

Location: The Underground Disco

Job: Tattoo artist and nightclub bouncer

Likes: Red ink, beefy biceps, rocking dance routines

Bubba is a monster of many talents. This big guy is terror-rifically tough by night, as the bouncer of The Underground Disco, Monstro City's trendiest club. But by day, Bubba is a gentle genius, tattooing his creative works of art onto the bodies of the City's more daring furless monsters.

Bubba's bared teeth make him look scary, but he's actually a gentle giant.

Disco diva

Hulking Bubba is surprisingly light on his feet. He practices his moves at home with his Dance Dance Roarvolution machine.

Bubba's muscly arms are covered in tattoos that he designed himself.

Great big show-off

Bubba is a truly Moshi-tabulous artist—both in the tattoo parlor and on the dance floor. The monsters of Moshi City already love his original tattoo designs, but Bubba hopes to wow them with his disco shapes at the next big dance-off at the Disco.

As a bouncer, Bubba always has to dress to impress.

27

BUG

Bug is his name, backflipping and bugging monsters is his game! It's best not to mention Bug around Colonel Catcher, the flutterby collector, because he has to put up with Bug's annoying antics every day. Just as the Colonel is about to close in on a rare flutterby specimen, boisterous Bug backflips into his net, scaring away the prey. What a bothersome Bug!

Best Furry Friend
Bug has a loyal friend in his BFF, Ratty. The rascally rat often gives his buddy a piggyback ride when Bug's short legs are tired from his mischievous antics.

The fins on Bug's head help him do goopendous backflips!

DATA FILE
Often spotted: Flutterby Field and up to no good all over the City

Best Furry Friend: Ratty

Likes: Causing mischief

Monster markings— distinctive big purple spots

Large bulging bug eyes

Museum mayhem
Bug and his pal Ratty go together like gooberries and ice-scream sundaes! Last year they hit the headlines of *The Daily Growl* when they were caught red-handed jumbling up the dinosaur bones over at the Unnatural History Museum.

BURNIE

Fiery Frazzledragons like Burnie may look cute, but it's best to admire these sizzling Moshlings from a safe distance because things can get rather heated. There's a rumor oozing around the City that the Super Moshis once employed these flammable Beasties to heat up their Moshi snacks. Well, it would save some hard-earned Rox on EN-ergy!

DATA FILE
Moshling type: Beasties
Species: Fiery Frazzledragon
Habitat: Mount CharChar on Emberooze island
Beastie buddies: Humphrey, Jeepers, ShiShi

Large nostrils for maximum fire-breathing power

Even with horns, Burnie is just too cute to look scary.

Flame-grilling
It's easy to find the fire-breathing Frazzledragons on the volcanic island of Emberooze. Just look for the flames, or follow the smell of ash-flavored hotcakes. Yum!

Little flappy wings for zooming around Mount CharChar

Gas guzzlers
Burnie and the other cheeky Fiery Frazzledragons love to slurp down gasoline. Several cans of fiery fuel later, the hiccups come fast and furiously, followed by monsterific flames that can fry fur from five feet away!

29

BUSHY FANDANGO

Looking for some Wall Bats for your crib? Or a bottle of Garbage Day Perfume for your latest monstery crush? Then come on down to Bushy Fandango's Bizarre Bazaar. This eccentric, adventure-seeking monster runs an Aladdin's cave of a shop, full of wonderful treasures from her travels to faraway lands.

DATA FILE

Location: Bizarre Bazaar, Main Street

Job: Owner of Bizarre Bazaar

Likes: Mountain trekking, treasure hunting

Holiday heaven
Forget roasting your fur on Bleurgh Beach! Bushy's favorite vacation destination is up in the freezing Yappalation Mountains.

Bushy keeps her blue fur-do bushy to match her name.

Journey to the back of beyond
Bushy has a monstrous thirst for exploration. When she is not working in her gloopendous shop, she grabs a backpack, fills it with Chocolate Coated Broccoli, prepares her trusty team of White Fang Puppies, and sets out on an adventure.

Splat-tastic! Watch out for this anti-theft device if you try to steal something from Bushy's shop!

30

BUSLING

The automated **Bustling** Buslings pass by in a speedy blur of blue. They are always rushing to avoid being late—although for what, no Moshi knows. These motoring Moshlings are far too tiny to fit any passengers on board. However, they will stop for a chat if you stick your arm out, especially if you're holding a diesel-filled doughnut!

Next stop please!
Next time you're hanging out on Main Street, look out for Busling and the other Bustling buddies. Wait a little while and three will probably turn up at once!

Windows and body are kept super shiny.

DATA FILE
Moshling type: Undiscovered
Species: Bustling Busling
Habitat: Blakey Hollow and Main Street
Often spotted: Happily motoring along empty roads

Out of service
At the end of a busy day racing around avoiding pesky bicyclists, Bustling Buslings park for the night in Blakey Hollow. They kick off their wheels, throw out any lost property, and rest up on teeny bricks.

Clear roads put a smile on the face of this tiny Bustling.

BUSTER BUMBLECHOPS

Introducing the ultimate Moshling expert-in-residence! What Buster Bumblechops doesn't know about these cute little critters is not worth the icky flypaper it's written on. Visit Buster's secret ranch—if you can find it!—to see the largest fangtastic collection of Moshlings in all of Monstro City.

Moshi-tabulous missions

Studying Moshlings often takes Buster to the depths of Potion Ocean and beyond. His watery explorations include being glooped by Batty Bubblefish and blowing bubbles with Songful Seahorses!

Hunting hat, with pencil and lucky crocodile teeth

Master of Moshlings

Bumblechops started collecting Moshlings using the journals of his great-uncle, Doctor Furbert Snufflepeeps. The legendary Moshlingologist vanished mysteriously in the Gombala Gombala Jungle. After mastering the three "C"s (camouflage, chase, catch), Buster learned how to nab even the rarest of critters.

Moshi-tastic moustache is rumored to twitch twice when critters come close.

Moshling "nab"-sack contains notebook, pen, net, traps, and moshiscope.

DATA FILE:

Habitat: The great outdoors

Often spotted: Lurking in bushes

Assistant: Snuffy Hookums

Enemies: Dr. Strangeglove, C.L.O.N.C.

CALI

DATA FILE
Moshling type: Fishies
Species: Valley Mermaid
Habitat: Potion Ocean
Fishie friends: Blurp, Stanley, Fumble

If you want to catch a glimpse of Cali or one of the other "kewl" Valley Mermaids, then swim on down to the newly opened Sea Mall. These ditzy Fishies love flouncing around the shops, gossiping about the latest kewl koi band, or chillin' with their BFFs (Best Fishie Friends) in cooling crates of ice.

Headband heart flashes whenever a Mermaid senses romance.

He'd be *so* right for you!
Valley cuties love romance. Forget Fishie-net dating—a Valley Mermaid will hook you up with a fellow Moshling. Take a translation book with you, though, 'cause Valley lingo is, like, totally confusing, and you don't want to end up with a fishy date!

STARFISHBUCKS COFFEE

Cappuccino-licious!
The day Starfishbucks opened its doors in the Sea Mall, all the hip Cali Valley Mermaids were lining up to get a table. Cali says they serve the frothiest cappuccinos and the seaweed sandwiches are goopendous!

Purple is the hair color of choice for all the kewl mermaids on the block.

Fishtail for flipping, flouncing, and floating in the ocean.

CAPTAIN BUCK E. BARNACLE

Ahoy me hearties! Meet Monstro City's top pirate, Captain Buck E. Barnacle. This barnacled beauty had a troubled start in life after losing both parents in a tragic shipwreck. A school of Batty Bubblefish took him in and raised him as their own—no wonder old Buck is completely cuckoo!

DATA FILE

Location: Potion Ocean

Job: Captain of the *CloudyCloth Clipper*

Likes: Collecting huge piles of loot, leaving messages in bottles

All paws on deck!

Cap'n Buck and his crew sail Potion Ocean in search of treasure on their ship, the *CloudyCloth Clipper*. They come to The Port to sell their exciting finds, including bubble machines and marshmallow pillows.

The pirate look is completed with a skull-and-crossbones hat.

Cap'n Buck rubs octopus spit on his fur to smell horrible!

Buck can see perfectly, but wears a patch to show his devotion to his one-eyed pal, Lefty.

A pirate's life

After the shipwreck, Cap'n Buck drifted out to sea. He met lots of kind and interesting sea critters, including one-eyed Lefty, who became his flood brother (or best pal). Together, they hatched a plan to become pirates. They built a ship, assembled a crew, brushed up on their pirate lingo, and set off on a life of piratey adventure!

CAPTAIN CODSWALLOP

As the *Gooey Galleon's* spooky skipper, Captain Codswallop doesn't let a teeny thing like being dead stop him from barking orders. If only he hadn't been so greedy, looting booty on Hong Bong Island, he wouldn't be stranded in the first place. But that's what happens when you're smitten with a paw wavin' kitten who just so happens to be cursed!

The *Gooey Galleon*

Although the *Galleon* is rarely seen, curious critter Gail Whale has reported several sightings of the ship and its gooey crew out on the Seventy Seas. Eerie Codswallop can often be seen haunting his private quarters.

DATA FILE

Job: Captain of the *Gooey Galleon*

Pirate pals: Jaunty Jack, McScruff, Mr. Mushy Peas, Handy Van Hookz

Likes: Pirate hats, shouting "woooooh!"

The ghostly equivalent of skull-and-crossbones

Monacle stolen from a one-eyed sea monster

Rusty old earring

Gross ghost!

Pheew! Grab a peg for your nose because Captain Codswallop is infamous for his terrible odor. Pirate legends tell of his fuzzy facial fur as the source of the disgusting stench. Some believe that his beard is made from enchanted seaweed, while others think it's actually rotten cabbage stuck on with fish paste. Yuck!

35

CAPTAIN SQUIRK

Captain Squirk is a Zoshling who lives on the planet Symphonia, a strange, outta-this-world place. Squirk is Captain of a group of Zoshlings who were sent out into the swooniverse in their spaceship on a daring mission to investigate an odd red star that had been spotted in the sky.

DATA FILE
Habitat: Swooniverse
Job: Captain of the *Rhapsody 2*
Zoshling crew: First Officer Ooze, Splutnik, Dr. C. Fingz

Zoshling emblem is made from Gloop-tonite

Intergalactic headdress worn by Zoshling captains

Mission impossible
The evil antics of the sinister C.L.O.N.C. organization caused the Zoshling spaceship *Rhapsody 2* to crash-land on Music Island. Captain Squirk had to seek Super Moshi help to locate the missing crew.

To boldly play...
Squirk is not only an intrepid intergalactic explorer, but also one of the top musicians in the entire swooniverse. The talented Zoshling is often found playing the spoons at the Symphonia concerts.

Special weighted boots for walking on alien planets

CASPER

Gift Island Roarker

Gift Island sits a short ferry ride away from the coast of Monstro City and can be reached from The Port. Visitors to this present paradise are sure to meet shy little Casper, the Island's gift counter. He's always happy to say hello—as long as he isn't busy counting at the time, because he's likely to lose his place and will have to start all over again.

Counting for a living
Casper has to count every gift that arrives on Gift Island. By the end of each day he is so tired, he certainly doesn't need to count sheep to get to sleep!

DATA FILE
Location: Gift Island
Job: Counting gifts
Likes: Visitors, new notepads, pens
Dislikes: Loud noises

Gift Island workers wear a hat at all times.

Number trance
1, 2, 3... 6... 375... Casper has to concentrate very hard in order to do his job. If anyone makes a loud noise near him, it frightens him out of his dream-like, number-induced trance, and makes him jump right out of his skin!

Casper has a notepad and pen to help him keep a tally of all the monsterific gifts.

CHERRY BOMB

BOOM! If you don't like loud noises, then Baby Boomers like Cherry Bomb are probably not the Moshlings for you. These sparky, spherical critters are easily excited, and when that happens, the crackle and fizzle of their fuses is loud enough to blow the wax out of any monster's hairy ears!

DATA FILE

Moshling type: Noisies
Species: Baby Boomer
Habitat:
Kaboom Canyon
Noisie pals:
Boomer,
Judder, Betty

Baby Boomers rarely go boom.

Bubbling over
Kaboom Canyon, where Baby Boomers love to hang out together, echoes with their laughter and booming voices. These Moshlings are so bubbly, it's hard not to get caught up in their excitement.

Fizz, bang, pop!
Cherry Bomb and the other Baby Boomers snap and crackle all over the City. Any Moshi who doesn't want these sizzling Noisies fizzing in their face should be ready with a cooling bucket of water. They should also avoid cooking goopendous foods like jalapeño poppers with dynamite sauce—one sniff and Baby Boomers will be banging down their door!

CHICK CHECKER

To blend in, Chick Checker wears the official Gift Island worker's hat.

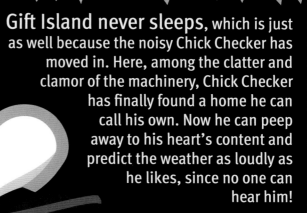

Gift Island never sleeps, which is just as well because the noisy Chick Checker has moved in. Here, among the clatter and clamor of the machinery, Chick Checker has finally found a home he can call his own. Now he can peep away to his heart's content and predict the weather as loudly as he likes, since no one can hear him!

Wish you were here

Chick Checker set up home at the very top of the Gift Island Postcard Shop's chimney. His nest is always toasty warm.

DATA FILE
Location: Gift Island
Job: Predicting weather changes
Likes: Whistling, catching worms

Long beak helps Chick whistle loud tunes.

Chick's cozy nest

Home, noisy home!

The cheeping Chick Checker used to live in Monstro City and loved peeping all day and all night. However, the sleep-deprived monsters of the town soon protested about the nonstop noise. After they put their paw prints on a petition and sent it to the MNP (Monster Noise Pollution) office, Chick Checker knew it was time to pack up his nest and weather charts and migrate to a place that was noisier than he was.

39

CHOMPER A D STOMPER

This chomping pair is often spotted grazing on patches of grass around Monstro City. Chomper and Stomper roam far and wide over the fields and parks, munching their way through hundreds of tons of grass each day. The City is proud of its turf-trimming team because they keep on mowing the grass until... well, until the cows come home!

Home sweet home
At the end of each day, these MOO-pendous munchers retire to their cozy barn on Sludge Street, to rest their aching jaws and throbbing hooves.

Chomper proudly sports two large pink horns.

This spotty pair are easily spotted!

Super-grazers!
Chomper and Stomper used to graze exclusively for a local farmer. When monsters began to get lost in the overgrown grass all over the City, the farmer gave this dynamic duo their freedom, realizing that their powerful chewing skills and monstrous appetites could solve the problem.

Little Stomper can gobble down just as much as Chomper.

DATA FILE
Location: Meadows, parks, and fields
Job: Mowing the grass
Likes: Grass, of course!
Dislikes: Dairy products

The Cheeky Chimp

Cheeky Chimps like Chop Chop have had years of stealth training and know how to kung-fu kick better than any Moshling. But that's just a part-time job. They're actually full-time jesters with a passion for playing tricks. They like to drop banana peels from the trees of Sniggerton Wood and then break out in laughter when some poor furball slips on them.

Splat-tastic!
A custard pie in your furry face isn't funny! But sometimes Chop Chop and the other Cheeky Chimps just don't know when playtime's over. Ha-dee-ha!

Big brain for conjuring up new jokes and pranks

DATA FILE
Moshling type: Ninjas
Species: Cheeky Chimp
Likes: Devising elaborate pranks and schemes
Ninja pals: Sooki-Yaki, Shelby, General Fuzuki

A long tail is good for Ninja moves and quick-swinging getaways.

Ninja bandana is the trademark of a cool warrior

Joker in the pack!
When Cheeky Chimps aren't climbing trees, they enjoy aping around the City. These jokesters like to play naughty pranks on unsuspecting monsters, like glooping their victims with gooberries. Watch out!

41

CLEM

When **Gift Island** needed a Roarker to operate the new parcel-sorting robot, the RoboDonut, Clem knew he was the ideal critter for the job. He loves his work and has been doing it for so many years that he could probably operate the giant piece of clanking confectionery in his sleep!

DATA FILE

Location: Gift Island

Job: RoboDonut Roarker

Likes: Listening to hip-hop music

Often seen: In the cockpit of the RoboDonut

Little Clem sits in the head of the RoboDonut to work the controls.

Extra-big spade for super efficient shoveling

The RoboDonut has long legs so that it can step over huge piles of gifts.

Donut power!

The RoboDonut has certainly sped up present-sorting. With Clem's skills at the controls, and the RoboDonut's long robotic limbs, this machine can shovel packages faster than ten Roarkers at once!

Clem MC

When cool Clem is not working on Gift Island, he loves to chill out at his apartment to the huge collection of hip-hop music on his M-pod (Monster-pod). He's quite the dancer too—this monster's got rhythm!

CLEO

After years of searching along the length of the River Smile, archaeologists feared that the Pretty Pyramids were extinct, lost forever in the sand dunes. Then one day a monsterific sandstorm hit the region. Out of the swirling chaos, there appeared a wondrous sight—the Lost Valley of iSissi and a tribe of these pointy Moshlings, including charming Cleo.

Fun in the sun
Cleo likes to invite her Moshi friends down to the sandy banks of the River Smile, to help her build some superb sand castles.

Pretty Pyramids are very friendly and love to wave at passersby.

DATA FILE
Moshling type: Worldies
Species: Pretty Pyramid
Habitat: The Lost Valley of iSissi
Worldie pals:
Liberty, Rocky, Mini Ben

Fashion accessories keep these Worldies looking pretty.

Down in the Lost Valley
Bored Moshis who fancy some desert diversions should head to the Lost Valley. They can paint pictures on the walls with Cleo, join in with the Pyramids for one of their famous riddle competitions, or go on a treasure hunt for some lovely lost sparkly things.

The desert sun puts a smile on Cleo's face.

43

CLUEKOO

Nothing gets past the beady eyes of the Cluekoo. Some monsters might say that the Cluekoo has a bit of a nosey beak, but if they want to catch those cute little Moshlings, then they're going to need all the help they can get! With outstanding observation skills, the orange-feathered Cluekoo is the birdie for the job!

DATA FILE

Location: Moshling Garden

Often spotted: Surveying the garden, listening carefully for movements

Likes: Gardening, cryptic crosswords

Feathers tied up out of eyes to ensure perfect vision.

How does your garden grow?

The Cluekoo perches in a tree, watching which flowers the Moshlings like to nibble. All a monster needs to do is work out the Cluekoo's clever clues and plant the perfect seed combinations to attract new pets. Moshling-tastic!

Tiny wings for garden patrol flights

Loyal lookout

Moshling-catching is a full-time job— just ask Buster Bumblechops! But busy monsters can't spend all day waiting in their gardens. The Cluekoo is every monster's BBF (Best Birdie Friend), keeping watch for any Moshling activity, while the monsters are free to play, shop and set out on Super Moshi missions!

Yellow claws, good for gripping branches

CLUTCH

It's a **monsterfically tough** job but some Moshi has to do it. For many moons, this friendly delivery critter has been lugging his heavy sack from Gift Island to Monstro City, distributing gifts to its hairy citizens. The City's monsters are a generous bunch, so poor old Clutch has his work cut out for him!

Dockside deliveries

Every day, Clutch collects his large sack of brightly colored gifts at the dock on Gift Island. He waits for the boat to take him to the mainland, where he hands out gifts to excited monsters.

Heavy sack, bulging with presents

Clutch should visit Tyra's Spa to get a massage for his poor old bent back.

DATA FILE

Location: Here, there, and everywhere!

Job: Delivering presents

Ambition: To win Gift Island's longest-serving employee award!

Delivered with love

Clutch may look tired and grumpy, but he adores his job. His back is stiff and permanently stooped, and he should have retired a long time ago, but Clutch wants to keep on making his special deliveries.

Delivering gifts all day can be tiring.

COCOLOCO

Grab your dancing shoes and go wild with CocoLoco and the other Naughty Nutters. These cracked nuts know how to par-tay. A couple of sips of their refreshing bongo-colada and you'll be conga-ing and limbo-ing the night away, just like a Naughty Nutter! Go bonkers!

Jungle party!
CocoLoco is... well, completely loco! This rowdy little Naughty Nutter likes to hang out in the Gombala Gombala Jungle, dropping down from the hoohah husk trees to party.

Naughty Nutters prefer bendy straws to straight ones, so they can sip straight from their heads.

Cracked coconut husk head full of tasty bongo colada

DATA FILE
Moshling type: Nutties
Species: Naughty Nutter
Habitat: Gombala Gombala Jungle and the Unknown Zone on Music Island
Nuttie friends: Pip, Shelly

Flappy paws are good for shaking maracas.

Musical medley
Naughty Nutters are musical nuts. Visit the little Nutties for breakfast and you'll be bossanova-ing while they shake their maracas. Several sips of bongo-colada later, and you'll be hula dancing by lunch, with a bit of ukulele playing thrown in at dinner!

COLONEL CATCHER

DATA FILE

Location: Flutterby Field
Job: Retired Army Officer and Flutterby collector
Likes: Flutterbies, of course, and his moustache maintenance kit

A-t-t-e-n-t-i-o-n! Colonel Catcher at your service. No longer touring Bendia with the Moshi Monster Army, this retired ol' boy has lots of time on his paws. He spends his days roaming Flutterby Field for fangtastic flutterbies for his collection, though you'll probably hear him roaring in frustration when he misses more than he catches!

Special net for catching flutterbies

Colonel Catcher still likes to wear his Moshi Monster Army pith helmet.

Moshi moustache

Since his army days, the Colonel has maintained his splendid moustache. Every day he grooms and styles it with Sneeze Wax from Babs' Boutique.

Long, bushy moustache is the trademark of any self-respecting Colonel.

Board of Genus

The Colonel has become something of a flutterby expert. Leading scientists from outside the City visit to see his monstrous collection and ask his advice about new flutterby species. Every time he catches a new specimen, he pins it to his monsterific Genus of Monstro City bulletin board.

COOLIO

Magical Sparklepops like Coolio really are an ice-tastic sight to behold because these rare, cool little critters are enchanted! When they're chillin' out, their magical creamy swirls sparkle and glitter to the jingly-jangly rhythms of cheerful nursery rhymes. And they love to chill in the snow —too much sun means they melt into icky gloop!

DATA FILE

Moshling type: Foodies
Species: Magical Sparklepop
Habitat: Knickerbocker Nook in the Frozen Dessert Desert
Foodie friends: Cutie Pie, Oddie, Hansel

Sparklepops come in three Moshling-tastic flavors. It's a shame they hate to be licked!

Cool as ice

If you can't stand the heat, come on over to Knickerbocker Nook in the Frozen Dessert Desert. You'll find Coolio and the other frozen Sparklepops chillin' out and sparkling in the snow!

Lick-a-licious!

The flavorful swirls of these cool little Foodies will have monsters drooling. The greedy critters should keep their tongues in their mouths, though; if there is one thing Sparklepops hate more than sun, it's big licky tongues. But Magical Sparklepops *do* like to cover themselves in whackcurrant sauce and crushed nuts, which are monstrously hard to resist!

A wafer bowl might be good for holding slurpy swirls, but it causes the Sparklepops to wobble as they walk!

48

COSMO

The Mini Moshulator

Cosmo and the other Mini Moshulators could give Monstro City's brainiest brainiac, Tamara Tesla, a run for her Rox. Give the Moshulators a number problem to solve, press a few buttons, and these mighty math Moshlings will have the answer for you before you can say "gooberries!" Just be careful not to press too many buttons at once or they might burst a battery!

Moshulators are happiest when they're beeping out fractions.

Math haven

Peace and quiet is just what a Mini Moshulator needs when tackling monstrous equations. And where better to find it than inside these drawers on Honeycomb Hill?

Number crunchers

You can always count on Cosmo and the other clever calculating critters. They'll be your BNNs (Best Number Nerds) if you give them an exam, especially if it is full of long division calculations. The more complicated the better, because Moshulators can calculate the cost of a billion gooberries in seconds!

DATA FILE

Moshling type: Undiscovered
Species: Mini Moshulator
Habitat: Honeycomb Hill
Often spotted: Hiding in drawers

These mini Moshlings like getting their buttons pressed.

CRY BABY

Waaaaaaaaah! This baby monster cries—a lot! He's actually a first grader, but don't be too harsh on Cry Baby when he's howling at monstrously loud decibels. The little critter just wants some attention. After all, it is rather dark and scary in those damp Underground Tunnels where he lives.

Creepy cell
Cry Baby isn't actually locked in his barred cell. He chooses to stay there because it's safe and secure. He has been known to pop out for the occasional quick cuddle, though!

DATA FILE
Location: Cell in The Underground Tunnels
Job: To cry!
Likes: Attention, cuddles, lullabies

Big vulnerable eyes for shedding lots of tears

Attention seeker
Cry Baby knows just how to pull on your heartstrings. One look at that sad, sweet face and monsters fawn over him. For a young critter who spends a lot of time alone, Cry Baby believes there's no such thing as too many people to make a fuss over him!

Small purple body still has a lot of growing to do.

Paws are always ready to grip the bars of the underground cell.

CUTIE PIE

DATA FILE

Moshling type: Foodies
Species: Wheelie YumYum
Habitat: CutiePie Canyon
Foodie friends: Coolio, Oddie, Hansel

Wheelie YumYums like Cutie Pie are the most goopendously yummy Moshlings in the whole Moshi world! These cakey critters are so scrumptious that they need to keep a constant watch for predators. Fortunately for YumYums—but less so for greedy monsters—these tasty Moshlings have four wheels for super-fast getaways!

Zoomtastic!

Wheelie YumYums look good, smell good, and taste good too—if you can catch one! These wheeled Foodie wonders have honed the art of speed. They fuel themselves with gallons of super-sweet cocoa, get extra oomph from their sugary sprinkles, and are topped off with a woo-wooing cherry siren to clear anyone who might slow them down out of their path.

Polite YumYums use fancy napkins to wipe their cute little mouths.

Turbo-charged sprinkles give extra power.

Lightning-fast wheels for fleeing hungry predators

Cake paradise

CutiePie Canyon, home to the YumYums, cuts through icing-topped cakes. Its fangtastic aromas are so strong, they waft all the way across Ramekin Plain.

51

DEWY

Meet Dewy, a scatterbrained, DIY-obsessed monster who runs the DIY Shop on Sludge Street. When he's not helping monsters select a rare Raarghly Bear Rug or a Gloop Shelf to display their knickknacks, Dewy leafs through *The Hammer Times* and gets inspired with ideas for fangtastic new things to invent.

DIY Shop
Dewy's store provides exquisite flooring, windows, doors, and shelves to the monsters of Monstro City. Dewy even designs many of the items himself!

Ingenious inventor
Dewy is most proud of his jet-powered jelly bean sorter, made from a plastic fork, a rubber band, a wooden plank, and Bangers and Mash! It was gloopendous—until it went haywire, dragging poor Dewy along the streets of Monstro City!

DATA FILE
Location: The DIY Shop, Sludge Street
Job: Owner of the DIY Shop
Likes: DIY, of course, and Slug Slurp Slushies

Dewy's wild fur-do is crazy and messy, just like Dewy himself.

Being a DIY kinda guy, Dewy patches up his old clothes rather than shop for new ones.

52

DIAVLO

Fzzzzzt! **Diavlo** is one smokin' Moshi Monster. You definitely don't want to get on the wrong side of these fiery little critters as they have very short tempers. They may be char-vellous fun and chipper when they're happy, but bug these little devils at your own risk and wait for a monstrous eruption!

Diavlo vs. Katsuma

Diavlos need an outlet for all their explosive energy. A game of soccer with a karate-kicking Katsuma is just the ticket. Let's just hope there's no fouling, or things might really kick off!

Crater head filled with lava

DATA FILE

Habitat: Monstro City (and anywhere in the Moshi world)

Catchphrases: "Sizzly-Fizzly!", "Smokin'!", "Fzzzztt!", "Char-vellous!"

Monster pals: Furi, Katsuma, Luvli, Poppet, Zommer

Hotheaded!

It's not hard to see why these little monsters lose their tempers so easily. If your head was filled with sizzling lava like Diavlo's, then you'd also never be sure when you were about to boil over in a fiery explosion.

Little flappy wings

All Diavlos have a pointy tail.

53

DIPSY

Pink, soft, fluffy, and squishy... ahh, Dinky Dreamclouds are so impossibly cute, you might just want to give them a cuddle! Teeny, wispy Fluffies like Dipsy spend all day floating high in the sky, admiring their own dreamy eyelashes and making cute tinkling noises. But beware, there is another side to these little cuties....

DATA FILE
Moshling type: Fluffies
Species: Dinky Dreamcloud
Habitat: Meringue Meadow
Fluffie friends:
Flumpy, Honey, I.G.G.Y.

Dipsy's rain tears make her long lashes grow and grow!

Cumulonimbus curls— all the cool clouds wear their fluff this way.

Stormy critters
Dinky Dreamclouds may seem cute, fluffy, and kind on the outside, but inside, they have thundery tempers (quite literally!). If you make these wispy critters angry or upset them, then they'll pour down with rain—all over you!

Dainty long legs

La-la-la-la-la!
When Dinky Dreamclouds open their pouty little pink mouths, it's like a choir of angels have flown into Monstro City. As for those long legs... surprisingly, Dipsy and other Dreamclouds don't like dancing, but they do love doing splits!

DIZZEE BOLT

Monstro City's Chief EN-GENeer, Dizzee Bolt, is proud to wear her special hard hat and overalls. No monster works harder to maintain the EN-GEN system and keep the City supplied with energy. It's tough work, but Dizzee swaps her wrench and pliers for knitting needles and dumbbells to wind down and relax.

DATA FILE:

Hangout: EN-GEN on Main Street

Likes: Arranging rip-roaring roar-b-q parties

Roarker co-workers: Ken Tickles, Bjorn Squish, Clem, Elwood

Hard hat with rotating blade for hovering in the EN-GEN room

MonstroWatts

Monstro City depends on the EN-GEN systems for all its energy. To prevent a disaster of monsterific proportions, Dizzee Bolt has to keep the MonstroWatts levels high.

Standard green and orange EN-GEN uniform

Powerful work

Maintaining the nuts and bolts of the EN-GEN system is a pretty tricky job when you've got only one pair of paws. So Dizzee employs a team of Roarkers to help her maintain the EN-GEN systems. What a gloopendous job they do!

55

DJ QUACK

Come on and strut your groovy monster stuff, the Disco Duckies are in town! You'll find DJ Quack and the other funky feathered critters showing off their Moshling-tastic moves on the dance floor, down at The Underground Disco. Try as hard as they like, no Moshi can resist joining in with these boogieing Birdies.

Disc jockey duck
Show DJ Quack a dance floor, a disco ball, and a mixing deck, and this cool quacker will play some gloopendous dance tracks and flap those feathers fast.

Disco Duckies shake (off) their feathers to the funky beat.

Super-cool red disco shades

Born to boogie
With smokin' shades on, feathers slicked and styled with orange sauce, and beaks glistening with glittery goo, Disco Duckies are ready to boogie! Their home on the TakiTaki Islands rocks all night to the pulsing beat of the latest tunes.

Feet are made for moonwalking.

DATA FILE
Moshling type: Birdies
Species: Disco Duckie
Habitat: TakiTaki Islands in Lake Neon Soup
Birdie buddies: Prof. Purplex, Tiki, Peppy

DORIS

Fluffle feast

Doris and her Plotamus pals think fluffle toadstools are fangtastic. These yummy toadstools give off a lovely strong smell of licorice, which Doris finds utterly irresistible!

If you go down to the Friendly-Tree Woods today, you're sure to see a Rummaging Plotamus like Doris. An obsession with tasty fluffle toadstools keeps these nosey, horned little Dinos burrowing under the trees. When they're not digging, Rummaging Plotamuses put up their dainty manicured hooves and scan the gossip columns of *The Daily Growl*.

DATA FILE

Moshling type: Dinos
Species: Rummaging Plotamus
Habitat: Friendly-Tree Woods
Dino playmates:
Pooky, Snookums, Gurgle

Fluffle nests

Digging, gossiping, and generally being nosey is monstrously tiring work. That's why these burrowing Dinos have to hibernate for much of the year. To guarantee that they have a nice snug snooze, Plotamuses knit their own cozy nests out of the few fluffle toadstools they manage not to gobble up for dinner.

Large eyes spot fluffles hidden in the undergrowth.

Big horn is handy for digging up tasty fluffles and dirt.

Plotamuses keep themselves looking pretty with awesome accessories.

57

DR. C. FINGZ

Dr. C. Fingz is outta this world! No, really, he is.... He's a Zoshling who works on the *Rhapsody 2* as Chief Medical Officer. Always ready with bandages to patch up fellow Zoshlings, the Doc can also read minds. What's more, fluffy Fingz can temporarily extract talent from other critters, allowing him to dance or sing like a gooperstar!

And for my next trick...
Poor Dr. C. Fingz was captured by sugary villain Sweet Tooth. "The Great Zoshlingo" was forced to perform his mind-reading tricks at the candy criminal's Cirque du Bonbon.

DATA FILE
Habitat: Swooniverse
Job: Chief Medical Officer of the *Rhapsody 2*
Zoshling crew: Captain Squirk, First Officer Ooze, Splutnik

Telepathic wiggle-stalk for reading minds

Dr. C. Fingz is always grinning—maybe it's because of those extra-large teeth!

Doctor who?
You probably haven't met the good Doctor yet as he's usually on a space mission somewhere in the swooniverse. But however far he travels, this fuzzy fellow can communicate with aliens anywhere—thanks to the wiggly-stalk-thing on top of his head, which gives him telepathic powers.

Very fuzzy purple fur

58

DR. STRANGEGLOVE

Mean machine

All villains need a super-fast car for quick getaways, and Strangeglove is no exception. His Baddielac 9000 comes with lots of villainous extras too, like terrifying Hidden Glump Blasters.

Mwah-ha-ha! The Doctor will see you now! He's evil, he's strange, he wears one purple glove—meet Dr. Strangeglove, the sneakiest, slyest villain in all of Monstro City, and a key member of the evil organization C.L.O.N.C. If there is a dastardly deed afoot, you can be sure Dr. Strangeglove is the evil genius behind it.

Twirly moustache and tall hat obscure this master of disguise.

DATA FILE

Location: Here, there, and everywhere!

Job: Dastardly deeds, member of C.L.O.N.C.

Previous jobs: Doctor of Moshlingology and Sinister Minister

Purple glove has all kinds of evil mystical powers.

Becoming a bad guy

Before he became the most-wanted villain in the City, Lavender Troggs (as he was once known) was a Doctor of Moshlingology at the Super Moshiversity. He turned on Moshlings and became truly evil when a Musky Husky mistook his right hand for some sausages and chomped it off! This terribly naughty genius has now set his sights on taking over Monstro City—and then the world!

ECTO

The Fancy Banshee

Woo-oo-oo! **Be afraid,** be very afraid. Not really! This is one Spookie that you don't need to be scared of. Ecto and the rest of the Fancy Banshees do look very ghostly, and they can drift through your bedroom wall in the dead of the night, but these glowing critters are actually very friendly phantoms.

DATA FILE

Moshling type: Spookies
Species: Fancy Banshee
Habitat: Parallel vortex deep within the ClothEar Cloud Formation
Spookie chums: Big Bad Bill, Kissy, Squidge

Cape made of electrified wobble-plasma.

Glow-in-the-dark

You won't hear Banshees like Ecto coming, since these wispy Moshlings don't talk, but you'll definitely see them thanks to their glow-in-the-dark capes. But be warned: NEVER touch one—the cape's wobble-plasma turns things inside out, and no Moshi wants to see what you had for breakfast. Yuck!

Banshees always float the right way up—they hate being upside-down!

Spooky vortex

Ever seen that swirling purple parallel vortex in the ClothEar Cloud Formation? It is thought to be home to the Banshees. Shriek "woo-oo-oo!" and they might let you in.

Luminous glow is said to come from absorbed Rox dust.

ELDER FURI

> Leader of the Super Moshis

Elder Furi is the ultra-powerful leader of the Super Moshis. Old and very wise, he can often be heard chanting "ohmmm"! Great mystery surrounds his past. Some say that as a baby he tripped and fell into the Well of Wisdom, and the rest is history. Let's just say Elder Furi would pass any exam on any subject without even trying!

Super Moshiversity
This clever monster studied Superness at the Super Moshiversity. Back then he was known as Younger Furi and his best friend was Lavender Troggs—who later became the evil Dr. Strangeglove!

> Mysterious staff can project the Super Moshi emblem into the sky.

> Flowing fur and beard show that Elder Furi hates going to the hairdressers!

DATA FILE
Hangouts: Super Moshi HQ and his hut on Mount Sillimanjaro
Catchphrase: "Respect your elders."
Enemies: Dr. Strangeglove and the rest of C.L.O.N.C.

Mountain retreat
Elder Furi spent many years in a remote hut on Mount Sillimanjaro, before returning to the City to train the Super Moshis. No one knows what he did there, but it probably involved eating garlic marshmallows and learning new languages like Furglish and Poppetonian.

61

ELMORE THE GREAT

What's big (and we're talking monster huge), super furry, and clumsy? Elmore the Great, of course! This friendly giant Furi is the tallest of all the Furis and has splat-tastically huge feet. Most Moshis have learned to keep out of the way of Elmore's monstrous tootsies when he is stomping around the City.

Celebrated monster

When the crisis of Elmore blocking the road was over, there was such relief that a holiday was declared. Now Growly Grub Day is celebrated every year with feasts and frolics, all thanks to Elmore the Great!

DATA FILE

Location: Monstro City and wherever he can fit

Job: No one really knows

Often spotted: Easily! He is the tallest Furi at around 20 feet

It would take a whole army of Roarkers to give Elmore a furcut.

Elmore could fit a couple of normal-sized Furis and a Katsuma in just one of his big hands.

Elmore the Clumsy!

Furis are known for their big feet, but Elmore's are the biggest—so it's no wonder he's the clumsiest. Once he tripped over and got stuck on the main road into Monstro City. The Grub Truck couldn't get through and it took lots of hungry monsters to get the enormous Furi back on his feet.

The biggest feet in Monstro City

ELWOOD

DATA FILE

Location: Gift Island

Job: Shoveling and sorting gifts

Often spotted: Sporting various injuries

Poor little Elwood! This Gift Island Roarker is monstrously accident-prone. You might expect him to get a sore toe or blister from knocking his paws with the spade he uses to shovel presents. But Elwood somehow manages to bash himself in the face several times a day. Ouch! That's gotta hurt!

Elwood has to wear a bandage all the time because he's always hitting his head.

Splat-tastic shovel!

Sometimes, when Elwood puts his shovel down to wipe the sweat out of his eyes, he accidentally steps on the handle and... S-P-L-A-T! With all the whacks to his head, Elwood can hardly remember his own name, let alone to stop standing on the shovel.

Elwood's shovel for moving packages around

Sweaty business

It's hard work shoveling packages on Gift Island. Before the gifts can be sent out for delivery to all the monsters in the City, Elwood has to sort them into different piles: big presents, little presents, and funny-shaped presents. He usually works up quite a sweat!

Monster-strong arms from all that shoveling

FABIO

Fabio is definitely one of Dr. Strangeglove's most dimwitted dastardly minions. Sadly, this doesn't stop him from carrying out the Doctor's sinister missions; he doesn't have the brains to ask questions! He just goes for his target, three teeth at the ready for his fearsome fighting move, the Triple Tooth TerrorBite!

Cakes, gloopendous cakes!
Fabio can eat like there's no tomorrow! He's especially fond of sprinkle-topped iced cakes, and will stop at nothing in order to gobble up their sugary gooeyness!

Perfectly-groomed pink coif

Vacant, dim stare

Fabio once tried to eat his own teeth, but he found them too glumpy!

DATA FILE
Location: Top Secret
Job: C.L.O.N.C. minion
Features: Three teeth, a pink hair-don't

Coif-tastic
Fabio doesn't have the brains for doing much other than chomping his enemies into pieces with his triple-toothed chops. The rest of his time is spent combing and gelling his silly pink coif into shape.

FIFI

The Oochie Poochie

DATA FILE

Moshling type: Puppies
Species: Oochie Poochie
Habitat: Uppity Meadow in the Pink and Fluffy Forest
Puppie pals: McNulty, Scamp, White Fang

A swanky Oochie Poochie like Fifi is the perfect companion to parade with up and down Ooh La Lane. These snooty fashionistas absolutely adore being pampered and having their fluffy fur trimmed to perfection at Tyra's Spa. Best of all though, the Poochies love taking elegant bites of the cotton candy they keep at the end of their pretty little tails.

Poochies collect designer hair clips.

Uptown Puppies
Only the finer things in life will do for Fifi, like designer handbags, fancy food, vintage lemonade, and pampering sessions at Tyra's Spa.

Poochie playtime
When Fifi and her Poochie pals are not sauntering around town, they absolutely adore running (daintily) around Uppity Meadow, or parading through Pink and Fluffy Forest. It's a delightful sight, but don't be tempted to pet these Puppies—they hate to have a single hair out of place.

A happy Oochie Poochie after a day of pampering

Fur is always kept washed, pristine, and snowy white.

65

First Officer Ooze is second-in-command aboard the *Rhapsody 2*. This shell-clad Zoshling has a very special talent—secreting lots of Cosmic Gloop, which the alien critters use to lubricate all kinds of cosmic contraptions. The gloopendous Gloop can also make anything grow monstrously fast, so Moshis need to be careful not to get it on their hair-don'ts.

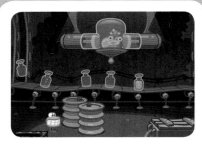

Alien abduction

Creepy C.L.O.N.C. agents were desperate to get their dirty paws on some Cosmic Gloop. They Zoshi-napped Officer Ooze, and placed him in a test tube to squeeze the gooey stuff out of him.

DATA FILE
Habitat: Swooniverse
Job: First Officer of the *Rhapsody 2*
Zoshling crew:
Captain Squirk, Splutnik,
Dr. C. Fingz

Googly eyes
on stalks

Ooze keeps
his shell on
at all times.

Stellar singing

Want to warble like fangtastic Moshling singing sensation Zack Binspin? Then you need to make friends with First Officer Ooze and get hold of some of his icky sticky Gloop. A daily teaspoon of this slime will lubricate your tonsils and auto-tune your vocal cords.

Squishy body
made of weird
alien gunk.

FISHLIPS

Glump

This icky one-eyed blob of badness is Dr. Strangeglove's dimwitted sidekick. It's not hard to see how this mischief-maker was given his name—just look at his large rubbery lips! They're perfect for delivering his dastardly move, a Suctioning Smackeroo! Moshlings, watch out!

Only one eye for looking out for mischief

Clump of greasy green hair

Calling all Glumps

At the slightest whiff of a new C.L.O.N.C. mission from that sugary villain Sweet Tooth, Fishlips drools all the way to the Candy Cane Caves where he awaits instructions.

Sealed with a kiss

With those luscious lips, you'd be forgiven for thinking that fiendish Fishlips would be a natural at singing. But most of the time, his rubbery mouth is actually sealed shut with goo! He does manage to play the trombone on occasion—until ghastly Strangeglove tells him he's not good enough, that is.

Slimy lips are stuck together with icky goo.

FIZZY

Lipsmacking Bubblies like Fizzy are great fun to hang out with; they're utterly unpredictable and refreshingly zany. One minute they're leaping about on their bendy blue legs, burping and hiccupping, and the next minute the bubbly drinks are sucking on mints while trying to lick their cardboard cups!

DATA FILE

Moshling type: Munchies
Species: Lipsmacking Bubbly
Habitat: CutiePie Canyon and Uppity Cup Creek
Munchie friend: Suey

Green straw for sipping fizz and releasing gas

Fizzy-wizzy!
If Lipsmacking Bubblies didn't have straws, they'd be in splat-tastic trouble. The gas from all that fizz has got to escape somehow, or they'd blow their lids!

Large lid to prevent spills

Big pink tongue for licking tasty cardboard

Lovely bubbly
Feeling thirsty for a slurp of fizzy soda? Then whizz down to CutiePie Canyon, because that's where you'll find that lipsmacking critter, Fizzy. For all you poshi Moshis wanting a more vintage fizz, then the Bubblies of Uppity Cup Creek are probably better suited to your tastes!

FLUMPY

The Pluff

You've just got to love the cuddly, big-hearted Pluffs! These dangly armed Moshlings are as snuggly as soft, squishy pillows. Pluffs like Flumpy are always cheerful, making them the best friends ever. These friendly Fluffies are so chilled-out, it's a wonder they aren't lying flat on their cute fluffy backs all the time!

Parachute paradise

Look up to the sky on a sunny day and you might see a grinning, long-legged Pluff, floating happily beneath a parachute and just chillin' in the breeze.

Pluffs look like giant cotton balls.

DATA FILE

Moshling type: Fluffies
Species: Pluff
Habitat: Cotton Clump plantation
Fluffie friends: Dipsy, Honey, I.G.G.Y.

Clean and tidy

Flumpy and the other Pluffs love to chill in the City, but the one thing they can't stand is a mess. At the first sign of untidiness, they're down at the DIY Shop buying furniture polish and rubber gloves. Ready, set, clean!

Long dangly arms are useful for clearing clutter and reaching cobwebs.

FRAU NOW BROWNKAU

This is a cow that you don't want to make moo-dy! Little is known about the fearsome Frau Now BrownKau. But one thing is for sure, though: the heinous heifer's C.L.O.N.C. pals are from the wrong side of the meadow where the grass is most definitely not greener!

Cosmic Kau

The Frau kidnapped Zoshling First Officer Ooze in order to drain his Cosmic Gloop. It's unclear exactly what the Frau and C.L.O.N.C. plan to do with all the Gloop, but it's best to keep out of the Frau's way—especially when she's wielding a ghastly Gloop gun.

Red lipstick, the Frau's trademark look

DATA FILE
Location: Unknown
Job: Working for C.L.O.N.C.
Features: Red lipstick
Bad buddies: Dr. Strangeglove, Sweet Tooth

The Frau posed as the manager of the Sandy Drain Hotel for a monstrous C.L.O.N.C. mission.

Hooves kept in tip-top condition for a quick getaway

MANAGER

Bovine brute

After a misspent youth grazing on grassy gobstoppers, the Frau left her hometown of StrudelHofen with monstrously rotten teeth to start her villainous career as the commandant of the Scary Dairy. A fearsome set of false teeth later, the Frau was ready to put her evil plans into action.

FREAKFACE

Mission: Big Top Ballyhoo
When candy criminal Sweet Tooth needed help on an evil C.L.O.N.C. mission, Freakface dressed up as a crazy clown to guard the sugary villain's Cirque du BonBon.

Freakface is the slimiest of twisted Dr. Strangeglove's evil Glump minions. This gloopy goon is Monstro City's undisputed king of drool. No matter how hard he tries, he just can't keep his big toothy mouth closed, so everything and everyone the wicked Glump goes near gets dowsed in dribble. Eew!

Clump of puke-colored hair

DATA FILE
Location: Top Secret
Job: C.L.O.N.C. minion
Features: Bad, dribbly, and slimy!

Greasy green and purple spots

Slobbering stooge
With his messy mouth, dimwitted Freakface has a ready-made weapon of dribbling destruction to use against Moshlings. Beware his Burbling Gurgling Gobstopper move! Things are about to get very slimy—yuck!

Always drooling icky purple goo

71

FUMBLE

Yee-hah! It's showtime! Rock on down to Bleurgh Lagoon for a five-star performance from Acrobatic SeaStars like Fumble. Death-defying bungee-jumping stunts will have you shuddering in your seat. Safety nets? Pah! These fearless Moshlings would rather crash-land than ruin the wow factor of the show!

Surf's up!

When they're not performing, the thrill-seeking SeaStars love surfing. At the end of a busy day on the surf, they pick up their battered bodies and stumble home to the coral reefs at Bleurgh Lagoon.

Pink eyes glow with excitement.

DATA FILE
Moshling type: Fishies
Species: Acrobatic SeaStar
Habitat: Bleurgh Lagoon
Fishie friends: Blurp, Stanley, Cali

Bright orange skin and a huge grin make this reckless show-off stand out.

Splat-tastic stars

Acrobatic SeaStars are not intentionally dangerous, but they are the clumsiest Moshlings in all of Monstro City! In between entertaining the crowds and high-fiving their fans, you'll find the tumbling daredevils busy gluing themselves back together. If you're going to hang out with these fearless Fishies, it's probably best you take a first-aid kit with you!

Five bendy, bouncy limbs are suited to stunts.

FURI

Moshi Monster

Harumph! Some say that Furis are the grouchiest, slouchiest hairballs in all of Monstro City and beyond. But look past the furry Furis shaggy mops and fur-rowns, because these lovable monsters are actually fangtastically friendly and just love to party and get down!

Luscious locks

It's monstrously difficult keeping up with a grooming regime when you're as furry as Furi. It's even worse when Furis get their paws on some tasty chewing gum—try getting *that* out of their hairy mops!

BFF (Best Furi Friend)

Waft some Chocolate Coated Broccoli or a steaming plate of Rat Tail Spaghetti under Furi's nose, and this huge hairball will be your friend for life! Furis like nothing better than a full-on feast washed down with lots of wobble-ade. 'Urp!

Smiling Furi—there must be some food nearby!

Furis hate getting their fur cut.

DATA FILE

Habitat: Monstro City
Catchphrases: "Haircut? What haircut?", "Let's be Fur-iends!"
Monster pals: Diavlo, Katsuma, Luvli, Poppet, Zommer

Furis wash their huge feet in the vast muddy waters of the Lush Lagoon.

73

FURNANDO

Now you see it, now you don't! Furnando and the other amazing Mystic Moggies are talented magicians who can make a sardine disappear in the blink of a cat's eye! No one really knows how the Moggies got their mystical powers, but the purring tricksters certainly aren't about to reveal the secrets behind their magic!

DATA FILE

Moshling type: Luckie
Species: Mystic Moggy
Habitat: Moshling Theme Park
Luckie friends: Penny, O'Really, Tingaling

Large magician's top hat, which is great for hiding sardines.

Abracadabra!
Furnando likes to wow the visitors in the Moshling Theme Park with magic tricks. With a simple "meow," these Moggies can levitate off the ground!

Beware the hypnotic eyes!

Look into my eyes!
If a Mystic Moggy asks a monster to gaze into its mesmerizing eyes, don't be surprised if the critter soon starts barking like a dog or ribitting like a frog! When not messing with monsters' minds, these savvy sorcerers like to try to sell them miracle fur tonic for their bald patches!

All good sorcerers need a magical cape to swish around.

74

GABBY

The Mini Moshifone

Gabby and the other Mini Moshifones are very friendly and helpful little Moshlings. If you want to make a long-distance call, send a text message, or play the latest games, these high-tech critters will kindly oblige. Be careful not to drop one or smear their fancy touchscreens though, or they'll switch off immediately.

Mission Moshifone
The latest apps give Moshifones all sorts of new abilities. When the Super Moshis were on a mission on Mount Sillimanjaro, Gabby was able to help them out—thanks to her laser app that melted the snow.

Techie time
The electrifying atmosphere of the mysterious Voltage Vaults is the perfect place for these Techies to recharge their batteries. Buzzing with the latest technology, the Moshifones gather to compose new ringtones and renew their contracts.

Latest touchscreen technology

Moshifones are chatty little critters. Luckily they have plenty of free talk-time each month!

DATA FILE
Moshling type: Techies
Species: Mini Moshifone
Habitat: Voltage Vaults
Techie teammates: Wurley, Holga, Nipper

75

GAIL WHALE

All the residents of Monstro City are eternally grateful to gentle giant Gail Whale, who spotted Gift Island one blustery day when she was out exploring Potion Ocean. This fangtastic find changed the lives of everyone who loves to give and receive gifts, and earned Gail a place in the Moshi history books.

DATA FILE

Location: The waters around Monstro City and out in the open seas

Job: Hunting for new things

Best Moshling mate: Kissy

Opposites attract

Gail Whale and teeny-weeny Kissy are BMM (Best Moshling Mates). Since Baby Ghosts can't swim, Kissy gently floats on Gail's water spout.

Gail bubbles with excitement from her blowhole.

Whale of a time

Gail's very inquisitive nature makes cruising around Potion Ocean and the Seventy Seas a constant adventure. She is always on the lookout for new discoveries. The friendly, easy-going whale uses her HAM radio to report each discovery back to Monstro City.

You can spot Gail out on the ocean thanks to her distinctive stripes.

With a ready smile, Gail is the friendliest monster whale.

THE GATEKEEPER

DATA FILE

Location: Entrance to the Super Moshis' volcanic HQ

Job: Gatekeeper

Family: His second cousin is the villainous Hatekeeper

The **Gatekeeper** was chosen by Elder Furi to guard the Super Moshis' volcanic HQ because of his powers of observation and love of keys. And the giant wooden watchful head takes his role very seriously; if he doesn't like the look of your furry face, there's no way you're getting in.

Super Moshis must insert a gem key into the Gatekeeper's head to gain access to their HQ.

Large wooden eyes are peeled for intruders.

Head is said to have once topped the tallest totem pole in TikkiHaahaa.

Head Moshi

The Gatekeeper works 24 hours a day and never gets a break, but it doesn't bother him. Well, when you're stuck in one position, it's hard to find somebody to share your leisure time with!

My lips are sealed

The Gatekeeper has certainly seen some Super Moshi comings and goings in his time; nothing gets past this hawk-eyed totem head. But you can rest assured that he will never reveal the Super secrets. He'd rather eat his own woodworm than break any rules.

77

GENERAL FUZUKI

According to legend, Warrior Wombats like General Fuzuki once guarded the caverns of Mount Sillimanjaro because it was believed that they never sleep. But now it's thought their apparent open eyes might just be cake tins that hide the fact they're dozing on the job! So far no one has ever stayed awake long enough to find out for sure... zzzzzzz!

Ninja skills
General Fuzuki is a serious Ninja who spends time practicing his stealth moves. Poor old Chomper got the fright of her life when the hairy warrior managed to sneak up on her.

Land of the midnight sun
If you want to meet a Warrior Wombat, head to ChillyBot State Park. It's believed the napping Ninjas live in the freezing wastelands, where the sun never sets. Be sure to pack your shades, a comfy cushion, and some cake tins as gifts.

Special helmet protects head in combat.

Ninja sword for protecting shiny valuables from thieves

DATA FILE
Moshling type: Ninjas
Species: Warrior Wombat
Habitat: ChillyBot State Park
Ninja pals: Sooki-Yaki, Chop Chop, Shelby

Shaggy red beard

GIGI

DATA FILE

Moshling type: Ponies
Species: Magical Mule
Habitat: Crystal Grotto near Copperfield Canyon
Ponie pals: Mr. Snoodle, Angel, Priscilla

If you've ever had the good fortune to meet a Magical Mule like Gigi, you may have noticed how they like to glide up and down, munch on goopendous cotton candy and hum carnival tunes. That's because these charming little Ponies are descended from enchanted carousel horses, so it's all in their horsey genes.

Unihorn is an ice-cream cone held in place with liquorice shoelaces.

These chic Mules keep themselves well-groomed.

Magical Mules inherited their pretty star markings from their carousel-horse ancestors.

Rainbow magic

Leaping fences and creating shimmering rainbows in their wake come naturally to cute Gigi and her fellow Magical Mules.

Great galloping Ponies!

Trot over to the Crystal Grotto near Copperfield Canyon to glide and gallop with these dainty-hooved Ponies. This is where they get together to graze on wild fluttercups and cotton candy. While you're there, these pretty Ponies may show you how to make the cutest hair accessory, a magical daisy chain.

79

GILBERT FINNSTER

Want to catch that elusive little Moshling critter for your zoo? Then pop on down to see Gilbert Finnster, the fin-tastic fishy fella who owns Paws 'n' Claws. The pawsome store is filled with all kinds of Moshling goods and memorabilia. Gilbert's an expert in all things Moshling. Only Moshling maestro Buster Bumblechops knows more about these little critters!

Gilbert's fez completes his eccentric look.

Service with a fishy smile

Gilbert's shelves are bursting with cuddly Moshling toys and huts of all shapes and sizes for the little pets to live in. He even sells Moshling habitat wallpaper to make the critters feel at home!

Fins flapping in panic. Gilbert is easily stressed with so much stock to sell!

Gilbert wears his elegant red robe to work in his shop.

Crack the code

Gilbert has always been interested in Moshlings. As a tiny tadpole, he watered and watched his Moshling Garden every day to perfect the art of attracting these creatures with seeds. Now he shares this expertise with his customers.

DATA FILE
Hangout: The Port
Job: Shopkeeper and owner of Paws 'n' Claws
Likes: Moshlings, gardening

GINGERSNAP

DATA FILE

Moshling type: Kitties
Species: Whinger Cat
Habitat: Sloth Swamp near Hopeless Hill
Kittie chums: Purdy, Waldo, Lady Meowford

Whinger by name, whinger by nature... Whinger Cats from Sloth Swamp do like to whine, especially if some Moshi pilfers their favorite melted cheese. Don't expect to see lazy furballs like Gingersnap roaming the streets. That involves far too much effort. And don't expect a wave—it would be a CAT-astrophe to have to actually lift a paw!

Cute but scruffy. These lazy Kitties can't be bothered to groom their fur.

"M" for "melted" cheese!

Sleepyhead
Whinger Cats like Gingersnap love nothing better than snoozing on a furry rug in front of a roaring fire at Buster Bumblechop's ranch. Just PURRR-fect!

Gingersnap got this scar after a vicious scrap over some cheese on toast.

Hidden talent
A monstrous rumor is going around the City that these moaning Moshlings are great at fixing things! Don't ask one to do your DIY though, as Whingers never turn up on time. They're too busy slouching around at Sloth Swamp!

81

GIUSEPPE GELATO

Next time you're in Ooh La Lane, be sure to pop into Giuseppe Gelato's Ice Scream Parlour. Mamma mia! His ice screams are outta this world! Talented Giuseppe invents his own flavors and toppings. His ice screams are so fangtastically tasty that they cause monsters to drool all down their furry fronts!

DATA FILE
Hangout: Ooh La Lane
Job: Ice Scream Parlor owner
Likes: Inventing new recipes and flavors for his ice scream

Monstrously styled moustache

Sleeves rolled up, ready for some hard work!

Beach treat
On monstrously hot days, Giuseppe takes his ice-scream truck down to Bleurgh Beach. Sun-baked customers really enjoy the refreshing coolness of his goopendous icy desserts.

Next!
There's no slacking in Giuseppe's shop. In fact, he's had complaints that he's too eager to serve the next customer. Monsters don't like being told to scram before they've even been served, just because they're slow choosing between toppings and flavors!

Large candy-striped apron protects clothes from ice-scream spills.

GOLDIROX

Blingo's Bling

This sparkling little charm is more than just a pretty face. As well as decorating Blingo's neck chain, wise GoldiRox gives the Flashy Fox advice on anything and everything, including his rapper lingo. Blessed with a silky-smooth voice too, glitzy Goldi provides the perfect accompaniment to Blingo's raptastic rhymes.

Blinging pair
When Blingo first saw GoldiRox, he couldn't resist her glittering glamor. The Flashy Fox found her dangling all alone from the rearview mirror of an abandoned limo up in the Hipsta Hills. Now he wears the blinging beauty around his neck whenever he can.

Fluttering eyelashes

A charmed life
Let's face it, dazzling GoldiRox knows how to look good! And she knows how to have a good time, too. When she isn't hanging with Blingo, this sassy charmer hitches a ride to YoYo Drive, north of Ker-Ching, to chill with her bling-tastic buddies.

Enchanted sparkling jewels

DATA FILE
Location: Around Blingo's neck or on YoYo Drive

Current job: Blingo's advisor

Previous job: Rearview mirror dangler

83

GOO FIGHTERS

Gooey-er than gloop soup, the slime-tastic Goo Fighters are setting the rockin' gunge world on fire! But be warned: there's a serious slime problem when these four monsters are in town. Excited fans have been known to slip in gloop as they try to get their hairy paws on the gooey boys. Splat-tastic!

DATA FILE
Location: On tour all over the Moshi world
Job: Musicians, gungers
Likes: Loud guitars, loud drums, LOUD everything!

With all those arms, Squint Beastford is one goopendous drummer.

On tour
The Goo Fighters say their gloopendous style of music is greatly influenced by the old-school gloopy gungers, Hurl Jam. When on tour, the Goos sometimes honor their idols by glooping the whole stadium!

The band's two gungy guitarists are fangtastic jammers!

Age of Gunge
The Goo Fighters were formed by Davy Gravy and Squint Beastford after a night of particularly sticky jamming at the Slimelite nightclub during the Gunge era. They then placed an ad in the *New Monster Eye* music magazine for two guitarists—and the rest is music history!

Lead singer Davy Gravy was once in the legendary band Bleurgh-varna.

GRACIE

Talented little figure-skating Moshlings like Gracie are usually found wherever there's ice. The Swishy Missies' sequined magic tiaras and graceful figure-skating moves will certainly dazzle any monster who's lucky enough to spot one whizzing past!

Dancing on ice

Swishy Missies know how to put on a spectacular ice-skating show. Moshis who brave the cold and climb up to the Frostipop Glacier will get to see some fangtastic twirling and jumping!

Sequined magic tiara could be the secret to the Swishies' skating talents.

DATA FILE

Moshling type: Snowies
Species: Swishy Missy
Habitat: Anywhere, but often on the Frostipop Glacier
Snowie buddies: Tomba, Woolly, Leo

SPLAT-tastic

On the ice, Gracie and her sparkling Swishy pals are super-talented skaters. But off the ice, they're anything but graceful. If you refused to take your skates off (even in bed!), "clumsy" would be your middle name too!

Heavy eye makeup is an essential part of the Swishies' look.

Swishies are never seen without their ice skates.

85

GURGLE

The Performing Flappasaurus

Ta-dah! Meet the magical Performing Flappasauruses. Gurgle and these other fame-hungry Dinos will put on a show you're unlikely to forget. They'll be pulling rabbits out of hats and making stuff disappear. Well, that's what they hope, but their tricks tend to go wrong. Be kind and clap anyway!

Abra-Cadabra!
Gurgle likes performing in the full glare of the Cadabra Flash over the Crazy Canyons. The natural show-off takes time to bow and pose for photographs.

Tongue stuck out in concentration

Gurgle's wings double as a magician's cape.

Tricky tantrums
Even though Flappasauruses are monstrous show-offs, they are super-sensitive when their tricks go wrong. They've been known to burst into floods of tears and burn all of their magician's props in a fit of fiery temper.

DATA FILE
Moshling type: Dinos
Species: Performing Flappasaurus
Habitat: Cadabra Flash, Crazy Canyons
Dino playmates: Doris, Pooky, Snookums

Tail comes in useful for tricks that need three arms.

86

HAIROSNIFF

Classic rocker
Arrrrrrgh! It's the legendary Screech McPiehole, Hairosniff's frontman. This big-mouthed, blue-haired dude is the only original band member left, but he's still screamin' out those tunes.

Calling all aging rock fans—the boys are back in town! Monsters across the City are combing their hair, squeezing into their tightest pants, and rocking on down to Main Street 'cause Hairosniff is performing its never-ending comeback tour. They might be old, but these monsterific rockers can still put on a mighty fine show!

DATA FILE
Location: On tour all over the Moshi world
Job: Rock band
Mega hits: "Don't Wanna Sniff a Thing", "Squawk this Way"

Guitarist Moe Hairy drinks a lot of wobble-ade before going on stage.

Golden oldies
When Screech and the rest of the band aren't on stage reliving their youth, they collapse in their cribs and actually act their age. It must be a relief to get out of the tight pants and complain about the price of boiled cabbage!

Scarf thrown by an adoring fan

87

Arrrgh me hearties! Meet Handy Van Hookz, ghostly pirate and shipmate aboard the _Gooey Galleon_. He's easy to spot with his two golden hooks. Exactly how he lost both his mitts is still a bit of a mystery in pirate legend, but a word of advice to all you wannabe pirates: never wash the dishes in a shark-infested sea!

DATA FILE

Job: Crew member of the _Gooey Galleon_

Pirate pals: Captain Codswallop, Jaunty Jack, McScruff, Mr. Mushy Peas

Dislikes: Finger food, gloves

Hooks are useful for catching a fish dinner for the crew.

Handy always keeps an ace in his hat for doing card tricks.

Handy's swashbuckling patch is hard to put on in the morning with no hands!

Handy hooks

Handy's hooks aren't so helpful when it comes to eating peas! But this cheerful old seadog doesn't mind his missing paws, because he's too busy using his hooks to swing across the _Gooey Galleon_'s rigging. Handy takes it all in his stride, though he's never quite sure what to do when Captain Codswallop shouts "All hands on deck!"

Into the sea

Luckily, Handy is a jolly sort of guy, because working for Codswallop is no laughing matter. Poor Handy is always having to walk the plank for not keeping the decks shipshape.

HANSEL

They look good, smell delicious, and taste yummy, but be warned: Psycho Gingerboys like Hansel are criminally insane. There's nothing appealing about these bad boys. Just take a look at all the "Wanted" posters in the bakery and sweet shop windows. Trouble sticks to these naughty Foodies like their fancy icing!

You can't catch me!

Follow the trail of scrumptious crumbs and you might find one of these tasty rascals. Unless, of course, they catch you first with a twirling licorice lasso!

Biscuity brains warped from being baked at 350 degrees

DATA FILE

Moshling type: Foodies
Species: Psycho Gingerboy
Habitat: Cookie Crumb Canyon
Foodie friends: Coolio, Cutie Pie, Oddie

Sarcastic smile

Candy capers

It's not hard to spot Hansel's crew of rough, tough Gingerboys because they're always hanging out on street corners, wreaking monstrous mayhem.
They fill their time with silly pranks—their raisin eyes are often popping out with laughter when they trip passing monsters with candy canes.

Icing is the only sweet thing about Hansel.

T - ATEKEE--

Fiery Castle Guardian

Recognize this face? It belongs to the Hatekeeper and bears a family resemblance to the Gatekeeper, but these two second cousins could not be more different. While the Gatekeeper guards the Super Moshi HQ, the Hatekeeper works for their archenemy, C.L.O.N.C. This hateful monster is the black sheep of the family!

DATA FILE
Location: Fiery Castle
Job: Gatekeeper guardian
Family: His second cousin is the goody-two-shoes Gatekeeper.
Likes: Blocking monsters' paths

Shiny precious stone

Fiery lair
The Hatekeeper really hates goody-goodies, especially Super Moshis who try to get past him at the Fiery Castle, C.L.O.N.C.'s HQ.

Burning green flame of evil

Thick, scowling eyebrows

Bottom of the pile
The Hatekeeper has always held a grudge against his virtuous cousin; when the Gatekeeper topped a tall totem pole, the Hatekeeper was stuck at the bottom and was an easy target for passing Puppies! Perhaps it was this lowly position that made the Hatekeeper choose evil over good and join C.L.O.N.C.'s sinister ranks.

HIPHOP

Calling all disco divas! Come on down to TinnyTone Boulevard and strut your furry funky stuff with the hip Blaring Boomboxes. Noisy little critters like HipHop adore old-school tunes and will wow you with their rockin' rhymes and the bangin' boogie-woogie beats that blast out of their speakers. Pawsome!

Flashy friends

HipHop and fellow Blaring Boomboxes love to groove on down to the beat with the blinging Flashy Foxes in the Hipsta Hills.

Tiny antenna for picking up radio signals

DATA FILE

Moshling type: Tunies
Species: Blaring Boombox
Habitat: TinnyTone Boulevard in the Hipsta Hills
Tunie teammates: Plinky, Wallop, Oompah

Control panel. Don't touch the record button!

HipHop's speakers double up as eyes.

Wipeout!

These dancing dudes will happily share all their tunes with you, day and night, until their batteries need recharging. That is, unless someone presses their record button. That will erase the Boomboxes' memories and they'll forget everything, even who they are!

HOLGA

Happy Snappies are never happier than when they're handing out their own snaps to everybody in sight. Want a furry mugshot of yourself, to hang on your living room wall? Then head on over to Shutter Island and strike a pose! Digital or film, monsterific color or black and white, Holga and the other Happy Snappies do it all. Snap-tastic!

Say "cheese!"
If there is a gooperstar in the City, then Holga won't be far behind, lens poised, zoom at the ready. These nosey little Techies will reel off a roll of film in a flash!

DATA FILE
Moshling type: Techies
Species: Happy Snappy
Habitat: 35 Mill Hill, Shutter Island
Techie teammates: Wurley, Gabby, Nipper

Twiddly knob to roll the film for the next shot

Flash-unit face is as pretty as a picture!

Techie tiddledywinks
When these friendly cameras aren't comparing their towering tripods or chasing after the gooperstars of Monstro City society, they like to focus on a quick-fire game of lens cap tiddledywinks. You've got to have a steady hand to launch a lens cap—one wobble and you're out!

High-tech lens to zoom in on those hot celebrities

HONEY

Funny Bunnies certainly know how to dress! These outgoing, well-dressed little rabbits have serious style standards and won't be seen in anything but the latest Moshi fashions. Hop into Horrods with Honey and you'll probably bump into hordes of other bouncing bunnies, browsing the boutique racks and texting jokes to their buddies.

Hip hutch
Funny Bunnies can't live in just any old burrow. Only the best two-story modern hutch in Pawberry Fields will do, darling!

Bunny business
Funny Bunnies like Honey love chilling out at Tyra's Spa. It's the best beauty parlor in Monstro City. They swap gossip and carrot cake recipes while waiting for their Slop! face packs to set and for Tyra to straighten their silky fur.

All Funny Bunnies have one floppy ear from listening to too many silly ringtones!

Funny Bunnies are smiley, chatty little critters.

Honey is wearing the latest Moshling must-have dress.

DATA FILE
Moshling type: Fluffies
Species: Funny Bunny
Habitat: Pawberry Fields
Fluffie friends: Dipsy, Flumpy, I.G.G.Y.

HUBBS

Hyperactive Hubbs, one half of the robotic inventor duo, Sprockett and Hubbs, is never happier than when he's designing gadgets, babbling about new contraptions, and skimming across the lab. It's a pity then that this bubble-headed buffoon wastes more time squabbling with Sprockett than getting on with his work!

DATA FILE
Often spotted: Whizzing along the floor of the C.L.O.N.C. Laboratory
Likes: Gadgets, irritating Sprockett

Hubbs' head is protected by a large glass bubble.

Monstrous machine
Sprockett and Hubbs created the Glump-O-Tron 3000. Dr. Strangeglove uses the terrifying machine to transform Moshlings into his evil Glump minions. Mwah-ha-ha!

Googly-eyed expression from staring at too many computer screens.

Tasty business
Hubbs is a very fickle robot who can't decide whether he should work for C.L.O.N.C. or the Super Moshis. All it takes is the offer of an oil cocktail or a circuit board sandwich and the cog-headed inventor will work for anyone!

Giant rollerball for speeding around the lab

HUM PLUM

Garden paradise

Stripy little Hum Plum loves her garden home. It's a beautiful and safe environment for her children to grow up in, and she can chat with Cluekoo and Scarecrow whenever she likes.

Hum Plum is an industrious insect. The little critter spends her days scurrying up and down the trees in the Moshling Garden, collecting invisible syrup for her hungry children. She stores some syrup for the winter months, but most of it is fed to her demanding little brood. Busy Hum Plum rarely gets a day off, but you'll never hear her complaining.

Wiggly antennae, used for tracking down syrup.

Distinctive pink and yellow stripy body

DATA FILE

Location: Moshling Garden

Job: Mother

Moshi friend: Cluekoo

All in a day's work

Hum Plum's litter is always hungry. They gobble down their gloopendous invisible syrup dinner like there's no tomorrow, talking with their mouths full and making a monstrous invisible mess. Guess who has to clean all it all up? Poor old Hum Plum, of course!

Tired legs, always scampering up trees.

HUMPHREY

Snoring Hickopotumuses like Humphrey are happy little country critters who enjoy the simple outdoor life. They love farming their land, but too much work makes these snoozy Beasties incredibly drowsy. Catching 40 winks under the shade of a wacky windmill and then a quick strum of the banjo will usually perk them up!

DATA FILE
Moshling type: Beasties
Species: Snoring Hickopotumus
Habitat: Skedaddle Prairie down in Whoop 'n' Holler Valley
Beastie buddies: ShiShi, Jeepers, Burnie

Large-brimmed hat, to keep the sun out of Humphrey's sleepy eyes

Howdy partner!
If any Moshi fancies mixing lazy daisy moonshine and can stand the smell of manure in the morning (yuck!), then they should saddle up and ride on out to Skedaddle Prairie down in Whoop 'n' Holler Valley. This is where the adorable Snoring Hickopotumuses live, work, and sleep—a lot! Zzzzzz!

Large nostrils mean loud snoring can be heard from miles away.

Home on the range
When they're not fast asleep, happy Hickos work monstrously hard on their ranches. A day's work includes digging fields, sowing seeds, milking cows, and mowing grass. It's tiring just thinking about it!

Hickopotumuses love to chew enchanted corn; perhaps this makes them sleepy.

I.G.G.Y.

The Pixel-Munching Snaffler

DATA FILE

Moshling type: Fluffies

Species: Pixel-Munching Snaffler

Habitat: Aargates—mysterious portals in cyberspace

Fluffie friends: Dipsy, Flumpy, Honey

With their cute fluffy bodies and happy smiles, it's easy to see how monsters are caught off guard around the Pixel-Munching Snafflers. But be warned, Monstro City's computers will never be the same again. Snafflers like I.G.G.Y. find cursors irritating, so the second they spot one—gobble, gulp—it's history!

I.G.G.Y. doesn't have arms to swat away annoying cursors, so the Pixel-Munching Snaffler gobbles them up instead!

Huge gaping grin, ready to munch pixels

Cyber critter

It's pretty difficult to locate a Pixel-Munching Snaffler because they're so unpredictable and they seem to sneak up on monsters before they realize the hyper little critters are there! Apparently, Snafflers whizz around in mysterious portals in cyberspace called Aargates, but occasionally these bouncy Fluffies are seen caught up in Monstro City's hedges.

The curse of the cursor!

I.G.G.Y. stands for "I'm gonna get ya!" No wonder—this Snaffler feasts on pixels and cursors for breakfast, lunch, and dinner!

ICKY THE GLOOP MONSTER

If it weren't for this giant-sized monster, Monstro City would soon run out of gloop! Once a year, on Super Glooper Day, Icky the Gloop Monster leaves the Land of Gloop and brings his precious gloop to restock the City's supplies. Everyone leaves buckets outside their homes in the hope Icky will fill them up. Splat-tastic!

DATA FILE

Location: Land of Gloop
Job: Keeping Monstro City stocked up with gloop
Likes: DIY shops

Sticky Icky

Icky is so gooey that sometimes he accidentally gloops himself, getting himself stuck to whatever he's standing near. Once he gooed himself to Dewy's DIY shop, trapping the shopkeeper inside! It took a long time to de-gloop everything and get poor Dewy out.

Giant-sized body dwarfs Monstro City's buildings.

Dewy stuck inside his DIY shop on Sludge Street

Giant myth?

Before Icky came to Monstro City, many believed that he was just a mythical creature. Not only does the Gloop Monster exist, he's so huge that he's pretty hard to miss!

JAUNTY JACK

Ghost Pirate

DATA FILE

Job: Crew member of the *Gooey Galleon*

Pirate pals: Captain Codswallop, Handy Van Hookz, McScruff, Mr. Mushy Peas

Likes: Fish sticks

Shiver me timbers! Jaunty Jack, seasoned shipmate of the *Gooey Galleon*, is always willing to lend a spooky hand to any landlubbers in need of his seafaring experience. They should probably bring a clothespin for their noses though, as he's rather stinky on account of the pickled eggs that he keeps under his hat.

Paper hat is unique among pirates.

Jack's hat

Jaunty Jack is not like most pirates. This salty seadog would rather keep his soggy paper hat than replace it with a proper pirate one. He's incredibly attached to it, mainly because he's named after the jaunty angle at which he wears it. And besides, it looks rather like a boat, and what's more piratey than that?

Greasy spots from eating too many pickled eggs

Despite the patch, it's not known if Jack has actually lost an eye.

Jack to the rescue!

Despite having a bounty placed on his head from a misdemeanor long ago, Jack is an agreeable pirate. He enjoys helping the Super Moshis on their undersea diving missions.

JEEPERS

What's yellow and striped and hides in a green place? A Snuggly Tiger Cub, of course! These adorable Beasties might not have mastered the art of camouflage yet, but they deserve an A+ for effort. Jeepers and the pack of cuddly Cubs spend ages squeezing the inka-inka juice from rare thumpkin seeds to use as paint for their stripes.

It's a jungle out there
Snuggly Tiger Cubs live in the Barmy Swami Jungle. Despite their terrible camouflage, it's hard to spot them because they're very bashful and rarely leave their lush jungle home.

DATA FILE
Moshling type: Beasties
Species: Snuggly Tiger Cub
Habitat: Barmy Swami Jungle
Beastie buddies: ShiShi, Burnie, Humphrey

Stripes made from inka-inka juice

Velvety soft, snuggly ears

Cute cubs
Jeepers and the other Snuggly Tiger Cubs always keep their claws nice and sharp. This isn't for hunting though. It's because sharp nails come in handy for scratching their tails and for opening cans of swoonafish. These little Beasties like nothing more than licking old swoonafish cans, while listening to glam rock.

Snuggly Tiger Cubs' tails are very ticklish.

JESSIE

DATA FILE

Moshling type: Mythies
Species: Ginger McMoshling
Habitat: Loch Mess and McHaggis Castle on Music Island
Mythie mates: Shambles, Scarlet O'Haira, Long Beard

Travel to Loch Mess on a misty morning and a merry sight will greet your eyes. The energetic Ginger McMoshlings perform a wee jig whenever they hear the drone of sagpipes drifting across the glens. Jessie and the clan fling their wee green limbs around wildly and end their performance by ripping off their fake red beards, which they then wear as kilts!

Traditional sagpipe-player hat

Fake red beard is glued to the hat.

A hole in one?
Jessie likes to play golf with the other highland Beasties. They gather near the ancient McHaggis Castle on Music Island to tee off.

McMoshling Mythies
It's said Ginger McMoshlings like Jessie resemble mini Jabbersauruses, ancient beasts that once wandered the Moshi world. McMoshlings are also thought to be distant descendants of the legendary mythical beastie, the Sock Less Monster. The plaid-clad Gingers are always hoping for a glimpse of their ol' relative Socky in Loch Mess!

101

JUDDER

Unhinged Jackhammers like Judder are rebels without a cause. Once they've been switched on, these hyperactive hooligans need to be handled with care—or they'll smash up everything in their path! These crazy critters don't care if there is a road to dig up or not, as long as they can boing up and down!

DATA FILE
Moshling type: Noisies
Species: Unhinged Jackhammer
Habitat: McQuiver Quarry and anywhere there are roadworks
Noisie pals: Cherry Bomb, Boomer, Betty

Orange hard hat worn when on a job

Builder's best friend
Judder loves going out on a job with the Roarkers, especially if there are burst water pipes to fix. It's smashing fun digging up a road and playing with cones.

Handles for brave Roarkers to hold on to!

Jumping Jackhammers!
These jittery Noisies are extremely useful when there's a drilling job to be done in the City. Otherwise, it's probably best to avoid them, because the Unhinged Jackhammers can be monstrously irritating—no monster likes having their teeth rattled in their furry heads!

Metal chisel for breaking up roads

KATSUMA

Katsumas are friendly but big-headed little monsters who love to be tickled. They look super-cute with big doe eyes, floppy ears, and fluffy tails, but they can be fearless fighting machines if they're angry! Highly trained in martial arts, karate-chopping Katsumas are all claws, jaws, and lightning-fast paws! Choptastic!

Time out
Being a cool karate expert is hot work. Clawsome Katsumas take regular breaks and sip on thirst-quenching energy drinks.

Heavily-styled tuft of hair

Sharp little teeth are great for nibbling Katsuma Krunch cereal.

Katsumas can take any monster down with a swish of their large stripy tails.

DATA FILE
Habitat: Monstro City
Catchphrases: "Clawsome!", "Pawsome!", "Choptastic!"
Monster mates: Diavlo, Furi, Luvli, Poppet, Zommer

Fashion followers
When Katsumas aren't perfecting their chops and kicks, they like to hop down to Sludge Street to pick out the latest fangtastic fashions at Katsuma Klothes. These style-conscious critters love accessories that enhance their look without restricting their moves—for example, stylish sneakers or sweatbands to keep the sweat from their paws.

KEN TICKLES

Ken Tickles, one of EN-GEN's hardest workers, is not a happy monster. His drilling is perfect, and he has dug up more roads than he has had bowls of hot gloop soup, but still no Moshi notices him. With his three eyes, Ken sees everything—especially if colleagues take a permanent lunch break....

Monsters at work!

Even Ken has forgotten how long he has been drilling the road outside *The Daily Growl* offices! Maybe if fellow Roarker, Bjorn Squish, stopped eating sandwiches, they'd get the job done!

All that drilling has left Ken hard of hearing.

Three eyes are better than one... that's if they stop jiggling around after all that drilling!

DATA FILE

Location: Main Street
Job: Roarker for EN-GEN
Roarker co-workers: Bjorn Squish, Dizzee Bolt

Time out

All work and no play makes poor ol' Ken a dull monster. After a hard day of drilling, he just wants to sink into his Yukea tentacle chair with a bottle of toad soda and a bowl of silly chili.

Blue Roarker coveralls protect Ken's fur from road grit.

KISSY

Woo-ooh-ooh! Don't worry, you can stop quaking in your furry boots, this is one Spookie that, quite frankly, is just NOT that scary! Baby Ghosts do try to be ghoulish and ghost-like, but when you're as cute as Kissy and her shy Baby friends, you're about as frightening as a fluffy heart-shaped cushion!

In a pickle

In the Okay-ish Lands, on the outskirts of Monstro City, lies an abandoned Harem Scarum pickling plant. Baby Ghosts live in the not-so-spookie pink plasma clouds that hover above it.

A pretty pink bow completes Kissy's cute outfit.

DATA FILE
Moshling type: Spookies
Species: Baby Ghost
Habitat: Plasma clouds above Okay-ish Lands
Spookie chums: Big Bad Bill, Ecto, Squidge
Best friend: Gail Whale

Perfectly rosy cheeks

Pretty in pink
Baby Ghosts are probably more scared of you than you are of them. If you breathe near one—poof!—it'll evaporate into thin air. Kissy and her pals prefer cuddling fluffy poodles, dressing up in tutus, and reapplying loganberry lipgloss and false eyelashes to spooking!

Baby Ghosts would never go out haunting without their hot pink pumps.

105

LADY MEOWFORD

Oh, it's hard being PURRfect all the time, but Pretty Kitties like Lady Meowford are annoyingly right about everything. From way up in the High and Mighty Mountains, these fluffy felines like to look down their cute, snooty little noses at the common hairballs in the city below.

Musical maestros

These sophisticated snooties love classical music. They're also talented musicians themselves. You might hear their high-pitched singing echoing throughout the mountains.

DATA FILE

Moshling type: Kitties
Species: Pretty Kitty
Habitat: High and Mighty Mountains
Kittie chums: Gingersnap, Purdy, Waldo

Large head to hold all that knowledge

Large eyes with extra-long eyelashes. Cute!

Clever kitties

It's just as well that Pretty Kitties are fangtastically charming because no monster likes a know-it-all. The fact is, Lady Meowford and her feline friends can do anything they turn their paws to, from skiing and lacrosse, to mastering multiple monster languages!

Sophisticated, stylish dress

LEFTY

One-eyed Sailor

One-eyed spy
At the top of Cap'n Buck's ship, the *CloudyCloth Clipper*, Lefty keeps his one very large eye out for interesting new islands to explore for treasure.

Not-so-nautical Lefty joined best friend Captain Buck E. Barnacle's pirate crew many moons ago. Unfortunately, Lefty had an argument with an aggressive seagull, which turned into a swashbuckling sword fight! The seagull was unharmed, but one-eyed Lefty could no longer balance on deck, so Buck gave him the job of lookout and put him in the crow's nest instead!

Arm for shading his eye from the sun

Spotty bandana—it's pirate chic, me hearties!

DATA FILE
Hangout: The crow's nest of the *CloudyCloth Clipper*

Catchphrase: "Eye, eye, Cap'n"

Likes: Playing eye spy

Often spotted: Looking through his telescope

Seafaring life
Lefty thinks of Cap'n Buck and the rest of his seaworthy crew as family. They all enjoy sailing the Seventy Seas together, searching for treasure, singing (out-of-tune) sea shanties, and shouting "Ahoy there!" and "Land ho!" whenever they get the chance.

No one's quite sure how many tentacles Lefty had before his run-in with the seagull.

LENNY LARD

Inner Tube Rider

When **Lenny Lard** isn't relaxing and watching the watery world go by, he has a seriously silly time playing in the sea. Ever since he was challenged by his classmates, it's been his wonderfully wet wish to become the first youth diver to plunge into Potion Ocean!

Lightning Lenny!
Having invented a watery version of the high jump, Lenny Lard can duck down under his inner tube and propel himself out of the water with super-splashing speed! Cap'n Buck likes to watch the action from the *CloudyCloth Clipper*.

DATA FILE:
Hangout: The Port
Catchphrase: "Duck!"
Likes: Ducking and diving
Often spotted: Waxing his inner tube

Body of lard is not ideal for diving...

No swimming!
The most astonishing thing about Lenny is that despite bobbing up and down in his inner tube all day, he can't actually swim yet! You may think he's thrown himself in at the deep end, but he seems to be having a stupendously splash-tastic time!

Inner tube bobs up and down all day long.

108

LEO

The Abominable Snowling

DATA FILE
Moshling type: Snowies
Species:
Abominable Snowling
Habitat:
Mount Sillimanjaro
Snowie buddies: Tomba,
Woolly, Gracie

Nobody knows exactly where Abominable Snowlings like Leo originally came from, but they have been spotted on the snowy mountaintops of Music Island and on Mount Sillimanjaro. Somewhat lonely and misunderstood, these snowflake-munching snowboarding sensations are actually very perky and playful.

Snow place like home
Leo loves chilling out in fluffy white snow, snowboarding, making elaborate ice sculptures, and building monstrous-sized snowmen.

Abominable knitting pattern!

White fur camouflage helps Snowlings hide in the snow.

Ice to see you
Snowlings dislike yellow snow, but adore everything else about the frosty, fluffy, flaky stuff. These wintry wonder Moshlings dine on snow, ice, and slush, and sometimes even eat their own houses! Well, they *do* decorate their igloos with chocolate flakes. Yummy!

109

LIBERTY

Happy Statues like cheerful Liberty hail from Divinity Island. These loud, confident figurines just love to have fun. They spend their merry Moshling days playing games, chomping tasty star-spangled candy and big apples, and wishing on stars—or just about anything else that might make their dreams come true.

DATA FILE
Moshling type: Worldies
Species: Happy Statue
Habitat: Divinity Island
Worldie pals:
Cleo, Mini Ben, Rocky

Happy habitat
Liberty and the Happy Statues were originally transported to Divinity Island from a faraway place called Prance. These Worldies love their new home, apart from the rain that makes them rust and the constant flash photography.

Daydream believers
Every time Happy Statues make a wish—for fabulous food, a new dress, or shiny stuff—their sparkly magical crowns light up the skyline. Nobody really knows whether their wishes come true, but as they always have yummy treats like ice creams close at hand, it's likely that they do!

Crown is decorated with cute heart gems.

Constant supply of ice cream—yummy!

Never-ending wishlist

LONG BEARD

The **Valiant Vikings** originally set sail for Monstro City from the Fibba Fjords. They still love to sail the Seventy Seas in their longboats—at least that's what Long Beard and the other cranky old critters say. They're always telling made-up stories about their supposed courageous conquests, so it's really hard to tell!

Fangtastic fantasies

Long Beard loves play-acting with a rubber hammer, pretending to attack no one in particular, and reconstructing ancient Valiant Viking legends!

Broken helmet horn to make Long Beard look like he's been in a mighty battle!

DATA FILE

Moshling type: Mythies
Species: Valiant Viking
Habitat: The Seventy Seas
Mythie mates: Shambles, Jessie, Scarlet O'Haira

Very long beard

Look beneath a Valiant Viking's considerable facial fur and you might spot the remains of their pickled herring snack. When they're not looting their lunch from the sea or crafting new stories, Vikings like to listen to heavy metal. These brave old Moshlings have surprising tastes!

Strong shield to fend off fictional foes

Rubber replica of an ancient Viking weapon

LUVLI

Luvlis are absolutely fluterly amazing, with oodles of magical hokery pokery and a glittery star on top! These sparkly monsters think of others as mere mortals who they love to dazzle. No Moshi is ever sure whether Luvlis have put a spell on them, or if lovely Luvlis are just naturally charming! Moshi-cadabra!

DATA FILE

Habitat: Monstro City
Catchphrases: "Greetings mortals!", "Hokery pokery!"
Monster mates: Diavlo, Furi, Katsuma, Poppet, Zommer

Sweet, heart-shaped face

Star-sprinkled magic wand

Magical moves
Luvlis make great gymnasts. Flapping their dainty little wings in the air, these cute critters adore spiraling twirly, wirly ribbons in pretty patterns.

Conjuring capers
Luvlis just love giving Monstro City's residents glittery goosebumps with their magical powers. They use their star-tipped conjuring stems to create all kinds of fangtastic spells!

Delicate wings for graceful flying

MAVIS

When you first see the *Gooey Galleon*, you might be fooled into thinking Mavis is just a wooden sculpture on the front of the spooky ship. But this enchanted carved critter has experienced a lot in her long seafaring life. In fact, Mavis is so old that she even remembers a time before the crew turned into ghost pirates!

DATA FILE

Hangout: On the Ghost Pirates' *Gooey Galleon*

Hobbies: Swiping tasty fish out of the sea

Often spotted: Appearing spookily through the fog

Ears pricked to listen out for other ships

Beautifully sculpted unicorn's horn

Long neck, great for reaching down into the sea.

Spooky sea shanties

Mavis doesn't talk much. She's too busy creating an eerie atmosphere on deck by humming sinister songs. What a creepy carving! She also enjoys bobbing her head up and down in the sea, looking for unsuspecting sardines to snack on. Yum!

Haunting the seas

Mavis moves effortlessly through the darkness, taking the *Gooey Galleon* headfirst into action.

MAX VOLUME

With his super-amped boom box permanently by his side, Max Volume knows exactly how to shake the room, the street, and The Underground Disco dance floor. The volume on his sound system is stuck on super-loud, so when you see him, be prepared to make some noise—just so he can hear you!

Bust a move
Challenge Max Volume to a dance-off and you may find yourself spinning on your head! With his pumped-up energy and cool moves, you'd better be good to beat this back-breakdancing bopper!

As Max rocks, his cap bobs up and down!

A boom box is the ultimate shoulder accessory.

DATA FILE
Hangout: Outside DIY Shop/ Games Starcade on Sludge Street
Catchphrase: "Boom!"
Likes: Beep-boppin' and hoppin'

MonSTAR
Max's funky street style speaks volumes—literally! His groovester's threads and squeaky clean "pump-that-bass" pumps made him hip enough for an on-street star appearance in Zack Binspin's music video *Moptop Tweenybop (My Hair's Too Long)*.

McNULTY

The Undercover YapYap

Psst! **Want to hear** something interesting? Cute Undercover YapYaps like McNulty love putting their wet noses in every Moshi's business! Originally from Sherlock Nook just south of Waggytail Hollow, these inquisitive pooches spend their time sniffing out secrets, sifting through stuff, and whispering tidbits of information to passersby!

Curious canine crew

With their nosey natures, daring doggy detectives like McNulty have a keen sense of adventure, and often find themselves in dog-hair-raising situations!

Nothing ruffles this cuddly fur.

Ears prick up to listen for clues.

DATA FILE
Moshling type: Puppies
Species: Undercover YapYap
Likes: Duping, snooping
Puppie pals: Fifi, Scamp, White Fang

Undercover pups

YapYaps love disguising themselves. Watch out for their tails though—they wag so much, they always give themselves away! When not on mysterious mutt missions, these cute doggies love getting their paws on the latest gadgets and gizmos, but they absolutely hate finding muddy paw prints indoors.

Incredibly waggy tail

115

McSCRUFF

Pesky pirate McScruff is a badly behaved salty scallywag! This boisterous buccaneer is the *Gooey Galleon*'s resident practical joker, who doesn't know when to stop annoying his shipmates. Luckily, he's also a bit of a scaredy-ghost, so the crew get their revenge by making him jump out of his blue, squelchy skin!

Look out!
McScruff likes to hover high up in the spooky ship's crow's nest, where he keeps a lookout for potential pranks to play and trouble to cause!

Bandana completes the scruffy pirate look.

Rusty earring

Ye olde rotten teeth!

Staying afloat
Despite being a seaborne ghost, McScruff can't swim a stroke without his armbands, so he's understandably very nervous about walking the plank! When he's not busy playing tricks onboard the ship, he also plays a mean accordion.

DATA FILE

Job: Crew member of the *Gooey Galleon*

Pirate pals:
Captain Codswallop, Jaunty Jack, Mr. Mushy Peas, Handy Van Hookz

Often spotted:
Blowing up his armbands

MINI BEN

The Teeny TickTock

Bells chime on the hour, every hour.

Tally-ho, chaps! Dandy Mini Ben and fellow Teeny TickTocks are posh and incredibly noisy Moshlings, who love chiming away like clockwork! Frightfully eccentric in every way imaginable, TickTocks like talking about the weather, and swaying to and fro to make their bells go "CLONG!"

Clock fixed to Monstro City Mean Time.

Classy clonging
TickTocks are very traditional. They spend their leisure time waxing their moustaches, munching soggy cucumber sandwiches, and asking what the time is. This may seem strange, but these timely timekeepers can't see the clocks on their own heads!

Slurp, slurp!
Righty o', it's time for a cup o' tea! Mini Ben loves caviar canapés, washed down with a dainty, delicious cup of hot sweet tea. Don't mind if you do!

DATA FILE
Moshling type: Worldies
Species: Teeny TickTock
Habitat: The foggy river banks near Westmonster Abbey
Worldie pals:
Liberty, Cleo, Rocky

Terribly traditional 'tash!

MIZZ SNOOTS

The winner of a number of "Mizz Monstro City" beauty contests and a scholarship to the exclusive OxSnout University, hoity-toity Mizz Snoots has always held her head up a little higher than those around her. Head to the monstrously exquisite Horrods and Mizz Snoots will help you with all your shopping needs.

DATA FILE
Hangout: Horrods
Catchphrase: "Good day!"
Likes: Shopping, powdering her beak
Often spotted: In all the right places

Designer bow hair accessory

Eyelashes flutter faster than flutterbies.

Always dressed in the latest fashions, Mizz Snoots auctions her old clothes (from the previous week!).

Moshi-tabulous style
Mizz Snoots perfects her poshi-Moshi look with ferocious facials, daily antennae polishes, and expensive highlights and hair-don'ts. It's no wonder this glamorous It-monster constantly appears in the Gross-ip columns of *Miss Preen Magazine*.

Superior shopkeeper
Horrods is the finest shop in Monstro City, where one may purchase the most extravagant un-essentials from one's elegant hostess, Mizz Snoots.

MOE YUKKY

With a name like Moe Yukky, you would've thought Yukea's shopkeeper was a very messy monster, but Moe is actually the cleanest critter in Monstro City! The reigning champion of the annual Slop Moppin' Competition, Moe has lots of glistening Golden Mop trophies, which he polishes profusely, of course!

Perfectly pristine

Head to Moe's store Yukea to purchase some fangtastic items for your room. Be sure to wipe those mucky paws before you enter though, as Moe keeps the shop goo-pendously clean!

Big eyes for spotting flecks of fluff

DATA FILE

Hangout: Yukea

Catchphrase: "Whistle while you clean!"

Likes: Dusting, polishing

Often spotted: Rearranging his shelves

Mukky yukky

Moe's shop Yukea has only ever been dirty once—when Dewy, who works at the DIY Shop, lost control of his turbo jet-powered jelly bean sorter. The machine pulled Dewy into Moe's shop, where it exploded! Everything was smothered in ooey gooey jelly beans—yukk!

Shoes so shiny and clean you could eat your food off them. Try it!

Smarter (dressed) than your average Moshi

119

MUS I MU TA

Ladies and gentlemen, monsters and Moshlings, introducing the most goopendous pop monsters in the swooniverse... Moshi MonSTARS! These Moshi-tabulous Roxstars really know how to rock the house, the stage, and The Underground Disco! Catch their number one song, "Moshi Monsters Theme," on the *Music Rox* album.

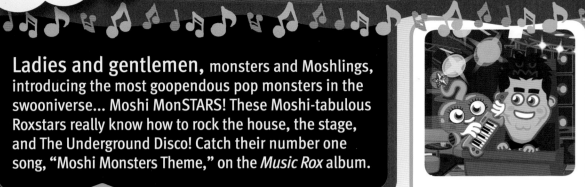

Growly mentor
Monstro City's talent scout, Simon Growl, auditioned the band members one by one, then put them all together to form one totally monsterific group!

DATA FILE
Hangout: Wherever there's a stage
Catchphrase: "Moshi Monsters number one!"
Likes: Rocking out, partying
Often spotted: Tuning up, very noisily!

Essential Roxstar headband to keep fur out of Furi's eyes

Fangtastic DJ turntables

Moshi beat!
The MonSTARS are smokin' DJ Diavlo, fur-iendly drummer Furi, clawsome guitarist Katsuma, flutterly amazing Luvli on keyboard, and stitch pickin' guitarist Zommer. Last, but not least, is cute Poppet, who sings her heart out!

MR. MEOWFORD

Mr. Meowford may look like any old fisherman, but he is in fact the Lord of Catberley Manor, working undercover. This posh pussycat doesn't need to work, but when he was a kitten he took up fishing for a school project. The young kitty found it so enjoyable that he turned his back on his pampered puss life and has spent his days fishing ever since!

The purrfect catch!

Meowford has become an expert fisherman, spending much of his time at sea. He can now haul and trawl tons of tentacled octopuses on his own, and make fish leap right up into his arms!

Sailor's cap is part of Mr. Meowford's disguise.

Talented Mr. Meowford can catch fish using just a box!

DATA FILE

Hangout: On board his boat at The Port

Catchphrase: "What a catch!"

Likes: Thinking of new ways to catch fish

A modest little boat for a rich cat

Rich kittie

Lord Meowford is super-rich, but he never spends his Rox on luxury cruises and expensive cat "nip"-knacks at Horrods. Instead, he chooses to while away his time with his fishing line on his boat at The Port.

121

MR. MUSHY PEAS

Mr. Mushy Peas, the peg-legged pea pirate, sails on the ghostly *Gooey Galleon*, trying to be as spooky as possible. However, thanks to his nautical, but very noisy, wooden limb, he's totally useless at sneaking up on his shipmates and scaring them!

DATA FILE

Job: Crew member of the *Gooey Galleon*

Pirate pals: Captain Codswallop, Handy Van Hookz, Jaunty Jack, McScruff

Often Spotted: Staring into 3-D space!

A different view on life at sea

Life in 3-D

This ghost pirate is hardly ever seen without his super 3-D glasses. He says he found them in the infamous Timeshift Trench under a pile of DVDs. However, the rumor on the Seventy Seas is that he actually pirate-pinched them from the Hong Bong Island souvenir shop!

Luminous green skin

Wooden leg, worn for effect!

Radiant rascal

No one knows for sure how Mr. Mushy Peas got his name, but some say it's because his ghostly glow is as pea-green as the mushy veggies themselves!

MR. SNOODLE

The Silly Snuffler

DATA FILE
Moshling type: Ponies
Species: Silly Snuffler
Habitat: Franzipan Farm
Ponie pals:
Angel, Priscilla, Gigi

Sleepy Mr. Snoodle and the rest of the slumbering Silly Snufflers love shuffling along in the slow lane of life. These leisurely lumps graze sluggishly on pumpernickel breadcrumbs at Franzipan Farm, and dance to Mr. Snoodle's latest dance craze, "Do the Doodle."

Big, heavy eyelids, ready for slumber

Yawn... yawn
Silly Snufflers have the power to make any passing monster fall asleep, which is handy for avoiding capture. When awake, they play ice-cream van melodies with their snouts... which often sends them right back to sleep again!

How slow can you go?
Once Snoodle was even slower than usual, so Buster Bumblechops managed to fit in his 44 winks before slowly chasing after him. The sluggish Snuffler had only walked six paces!

Super-snuffly snoring snout!

123

MUSTACHIO

Mustachio looks like a terribly important Glump, and acts like it too! Dr. Strangeglove's fuzzy facial-fluffed minion loves giving everyone their glumping orders through the bristles of his wicked whiskers. Mustachio adores his moustache, but despises Moshlings—he attacks them with Bristly Brush-Offs if they ever dare to ask him questions!

Dangerous disguise
When Dr. Strangeglove dressed up a pile of his Glumps as Headmaster of Super Moshiversity, Mustachio's face fooled the Super Moshis—until they cracked the case, of course!

DATA FILE
Location: Top Secret
Job: Member of C.L.O.N.C.
Features: Air of authority, immaculately groomed facial hair

Lumpy, grumpy forehead

Black beetle-like brows

Moustache is perfectly pinched to a point.

Looks are deceiving
With his thick, bushy eyebrows, Mister Mustachio appears to be a perfectly distinguished gentleman, but he's actually just a ghastly and dishonest Glump, with a permanently ferocious frown!

MYRTLE

DATA FILE
Hangout: Potion Ocean
Catchphrase: "Dive deep!"
Likes: Swimming, snorkeling, playing pool
Often spotted: Popping her head up after a long dive!

Splash-tastically skilled Myrtle is famous for her incredible sunken-treasure hunting skills. After diving down to the depths of Potion Ocean, this talented turtle surfaces with her arms loaded full of amazing discoveries! Her fascinating and rather random past finds have included a teapot, a shoelace, and a pool table. Monsterific!

State of the art designer turtle mask

Tough as a turtle!
Myrtle may be tiny, but she can carry heavy loads in the water. It's not that shell-shocking, as she has been carrying her house on her back for her whole life!

Googly eyes for spotting treasure at the bottom of the sea

Surf and turf
When Myrtle isn't cruising on the Potion Ocean seabed, she keeps her shell on dry land. She likes playing pool with her pals, showing off her trick shots, and practicing swimming on the table!

Home sweet home!

125

NED

Glump

Nerdy Ned appears to be a very geeky Glump! But don't be fooled into thinking he's harmless. Underneath the eccentric exterior and funny-looking goggles lies a ferocious fighting fiend! In fact, ninja Ned has all the skills needed to perform Moshling-mangling Goggle-Plop Grappies—yikes!

The C.L.O.N.C. crew

Ned is devoted to his master, Dr. Strangeglove, and the other cruel henchmen of the Criminal League of Naughty Critters. With his team of Glumps, Strangeglove is determined to take over Monstro City.

DATA FILE

Location: Top Secret

Job: C.L.O.N.C. minion

Features: Rough purple skin, nerd disguise

Wipe-clean goggles come in handy during messy fights!

If looks could kill

Naughty Ned's pair of goggles—which he wields as a weapon—are not the only thing to be afraid of. His evil fiery-eyed stare is enough to scare Moshlings everywhere and his temper is truly terrifying at times. It's best to leave this volatile Glump alone, and be warned: he's especially grumpy when woken from a nap!

Fake gold tooth replaces tooth lost in a brawl.

NIPPER

The Titchy TrundleBot

Titchy TrundleBots are often found clambering around construction sites or playing games in Quivering Quarry. These mini mechanical Moshlings are powerful and very versatile. Nipper's TrundleBot buddies helped to build Monstro City, and now they keep busy trundling across bumpy ground, reaching Rox in tall trees, and warning Monsters about falling boulders!

Nipper exercises his extendable arms with daily stretching and basketball!

Flashing head light warns others to stand back—there's a Trundlebot approaching!

Critter construction

Nipper is a happy, but hard-working Techie. This Titchy Trundlebot isn't impressed by on-site slackers like Bjorn Squish, who is always on his lunch break!

Body builders

Titchy TrundleBots like Nipper were built for building! They have flexible arms, caterpillar-clad feet, and an appetite for construction. These builder bots will never be seen brandishing rusty wrenches or wearing hard hats—they are well-equipped without them!

O'REALLY

O'Really and the other whimsical Unlucky Larrikins come from somewhere near the legendary Barmy Stone of Shamrock Bog. Unlike most Luckies, these magical Moshlings are poor, unfortunate critters, who would've run out of luck by now—if they'd ever had any to begin with!

DATA FILE

Moshling type: Luckies
Species: Unlucky Larrikin
Habitat: Near the Barmy Stone of Shamrock Bog
Luckie friends: Tingaling, Penny

Larrikin yarns

The luckless Larrikins don't actually realize they're unlucky; they're too busy looking on the bright side, whistling cheerful tunes, and making everyone laugh with their jokes and stories. In fact, these confident limerick-lovers will tell tall, tedious tales to anyone who'll listen to them!

Fake four-leaf clover brings no luck.

There's no point stroking this beard for luck!

Ever optimistic

O'Really really loves rainbows, but no matter how many times this positive Moshling finds the end of one, there's never a pot o' gold to be found!

OCTO

Cool cascade

Octo the watery wonder is just what you need on a horrendously hot day. If you're within squirting distance, she can cool you down with a nice refreshing rain shower of spit spray!

Port resident Octo is the ultimate purple princess of H2O! Eco-conscious and ocean aware, Monstro City's renowned water recycler uses her massive mouth to suck up bucket-loads of water, then spray it all out again, high up into the air! Splat-tastic!

DATA FILE

Hangout: The Port
Catchphrase: "Regurge and recycle!"
Likes: Bathing, showering, polishing her tentacle toes
Often spotted: Entering long-distance spraying contests

Recycling queen

All the activity in The Port takes its toll on the water, but fortunately Octo's spouting and spritzing is more than just a hobby! Oil from ships, scraps from fishermen, and even dregs of wobble-ade pose no problem to this purple cleaning machine. She sprays the water out as good as new.

Big puffy cheeks for water retention!

Octo's many legs help her get around.

129

OCTOPEG

Lumpy old Octopeg is so named because, instead of biting his nails, he nervously gnaws his tentacles. Because of this habit, poor anxious Octopeg has wooden pegs for legs, and has to hobble along the seabed! This eight-stumped fish-scoffing freak prefers staying put, resting his pegs and playing his favorite video games.

Underwater unwinding
Nervous Octopeg likes to spend time on his own. He's obsessed with video games and loves curling up on a comfy rock with a game of sunken battleships.

DATA FILE
Hangout: Under the Ghost Pirates' *Gooey Galleon*

Hobbies: Chewing his toes, playing video games

Catchphrase: "Gnaw, gnaw, gnaw!"

Hat is a tad too tiny.

Useful hook for scraping barnacles covers the end of a chewed tentacle.

Flabby fella
Octopeg spends his time feasting on barrel-loads of barnacles from underneath the ghost pirates' ship, the *Gooey Galleon*. Lumpy, bumpy Octo has eaten so many that he's started to look like a barnacle!

Peg-tentacled pirate

ODDIE

The Sweet Ringy Thingy

DATA FILE

Moshling type: Foodies
Species: Sweet Ringy Thingy
Habitat: Boiling oil swamps near Greasy Geezer
Foodie friends: Coolio, Cutie Pie, Hansel

Scrumptiously Sweet Ringy Thingies like Oddie love hot oil, as it is believed they were fried in boiling swamps of the stuff, somewhere near Greasy Geezer. No Moshi knows how these Foodies got their sprinkly spots or who covered them in pink icing, but every Moshi agrees they are the most mouthwatering Moshlings around—yum!

Mouthwatering sugary pink coat
Mouth always pursed in an "O" of surprise!
Fast footsies, great for running rings around Moshis!

Sweet temptation

Oh dear! Even carefree and big-hearted Flumpy the Pluff couldn't resist the tasty treat of Oddie's goopendously gooey pink icing!

Sprinkle showers

With their delicious dough, it's no surprise that these boisterous balls of batter often find themselves running away from greedy monsters. Luckily, they are able to shoot out hundreds and thousands of sprinkles at their predators!

OILER

Oiler spends his days looking for oil by finding underground oil pockets below the sea. He uses the oil to keep all the machines' gears on Gift Island perfectly greased. Without this busy sea critter, everything on the isle would come grinding to a squeaky halt. And with no gifts, there would be some monstrously unhappy city residents!

Curious critter
Oiler likes poking his tentacles in and around the Gift Island presents. He has refined tastes and loves to see what treats the Monstro City residents will receive.

Rocket-shaped head for drilling into the ground

DATA FILE
Hangout: Gift Island
Catchphrase: "It's oiling down here!"
Likes: Burning the midnight (and midday) oil, eating greasy food

Tentacle for extracting oil

Made for the job
Some monsters may think that Oiler is no oil painting, but his body is built for his fuel-foraging profession. He can move as quickly as an oil slick in the water, and instead of just burying his head in the sand, Oiler burrows his head *into* the sand. Then he extracts the icky oil with his tentacle suction cups!

Tentacle for applying thick grease

OOMPAH

DATA FILE
Moshling type: Tunies
Species: Brassy BlowyThing
Habitat: Polka Park
Tunie teammates: Plinky, Wallop, HipHop

Brassy BlowyThings like Oompah love tooting harmoniously in Polka Park with fellow Tunies the Squeezy Tinklehuffs. After they have tuned up in Windypop Place, you might spot this bright, boisterous band of BlowyThings marching along, burping rainbow-colored bubbles as they toot.

Hole in the head for optimum tooting

Playing for supper
When they smell the succulent scent of sizzling Silly Sausages, these musical Moshlings can't help but toot out a tune in excitement. Paaarrrp!

Polished to perfection

Shiny, tooty Moshlings
Although these symphonic souls love music, they very much dislike ear-piercing Kazoo solos. Oompah and the other Brassy BlowyThings are also terrified of greasy pawprints that threaten to blemish their shininess.

BlowyThings' feet march to the beat.

133

PATCH

Patch the seagull is a keen surveyor of the seas, keeping one eye on The Port for fishy characters and scraps of seafood left by fishermen. It may appear that this winged watcher has only one good eye, but the black eye patch is actually just a striking pirate fashion statement!

Plunging Patch

When not poking around in every Moshi's business, wannabe pirate Patch loves flying. He swoops and dives from great heights, beak-first into Potion Ocean.

DATA FILE

Hangout: The Port

Catchphrase: Something in Seagullian —no translators were available

Job: Monitoring The Port

Often spotted: Searching for scraps, stealing Slopcorn

An eye patch is the latest fashion in *Pirate Style Magazine.*

Bird talk

Patch's native language is Seagullian. It's a rather noisy and ear-piercingly shrill form of communication that no Moshi can understand. In order to give *Daily Growl* editor Roary Scrawl a message, Patch once had to play a funny game of wing-charades!

Wings can be used for flying and pointing.

Large beak for squawking and stealing snacks!

PEEKABOO

The Oakey-Dokey Hokey-Pokey

Oakey-Dokey Hokey-Pokies like Peekaboo can usually be found wandering the Wobbly Wood path, but they've also been spotted shedding bark and playing hide-and-peek in the Unknown Zone. No one is entirely sure whether these mysterious Moshlings are walking tree stumps or tiny woodland creatures hiding in tree costumes!

Sneaky peeky

Peekaboo and the other Oakey-Dokey Hokey-Pokies feel most comfortable in their natural surroundings, playing hide-and-peek and going for quiet walks.

Wide, terrified eyes

DATA FILE

Moshling type: Undiscovered
Species: Oakey-Dokey Hokey-Pokey
Habitat: The Wobbly Woods or the Unknown Zone
Often spotted: Collecting leaves

Leaves make excellent camouflage.

Joints are lubricated with linseed oil for easy movement.

You've been sapped!

Hokey-Pokies are tremendously shy and always on edge. Constantly shaking like a leaf and scurrying away, these panicky Pokies leave everyone alone. They squirt slippery sap all over anyone who does come too close, especially ramblers or monsters brandishing chainsaws!

135

PENNY

Jolly little Penny and the other Mini Money Moshlings originate from deep within Dime Mine. Nowadays, they are often seen jumping into wishing wells or flipping themselves high up into the air in Windfall Way. If you do happen to come across a Mini Money, pick it up and rub it on its tummy—it might just bring you good luck!

DATA FILE
Moshling type: Luckies
Species: Mini Money
Habitat: Dime Mine and Windfall Way
Luckie friends: Tingaling, O'Really, Furnando

Perfectly polished body

Heads or tails?
Fretful dots of metal like Penny flip themselves into the air when they need to make decisions. With all that spinning, it's not surprising these cute coins are often very dizzy!

Cheerful change
These jovial Luckies love jingling around in big pockets and being found by beeping metal detectors. But they live in fear of slipping down the side of the sofa or being plopped into slot machines again and again and again...

Legs made for springing high into the air

PEPPY

Rebellious rascal Peppy and the cool Stunt Penguin crew are obsessed by anything with two wheels. Sadly, they are useless at riding bikes because their feet can't reach the pedals! Instead, these pocket-sized penguins make revving noises, flap their stumpy little wings, and slide along the ice on their tummies!

Ice cool
Eager Stunt Penguins like to look the part by dressing in biker gear and sitting on bikes. But they look a bit silly, squawking "vroom vroom" and moving nowhere fast!

DATA FILE
Moshling type: Birdies
Species: Stunt Penguin
Habitat: Frosty Pop Glacier near Potion Ocean
Birdie buddies: DJ Quack, Prof. Purplex, Tiki

Smelly penguins
Sprightly Stunt Penguins like Peppy need to keep their energy levels up by guzzling engine oil and munching on fish. These reckless Birdies eat more than a hundred stinky sardine popsicles a day, which they keep hidden under their crash helmets. Peeee-yeeew!

Tough skull-and-crossbones crash helmet

Cool reflective stunt goggles

Tummy full of fish. Don't poke Stunt Penguins in the belly—they hate it!

137

PERCY

Percy was once part of Captain Buck's seaworthy crew on the *CloudyCloth Clipper*. But after challenging a pesky pirate to a fight, then backing out at the last minute, Percy was so embarrassed that he decided he would have to put his swashbuckling sailing career behind him—at least for the time being.

DATA FILE

Hangout: The rooftops of Monstro City

Often spotted: At The Port—on dry land!

Likes: Listening in on monsters' conversations

Pirate perch

Percy sometimes hangs out with his old shipmates, Cap'n Buck and his crew. Buck's pirate hat provides a cozy resting place before he returns to dry land.

Perfectly dry feathers

Large bill for squawking

Feet firmly on the ground

Beached birdie

Percy loves hopping from roof to roof across Monstro City. The rooftops offer this nosey pelican a perfect bird's-eye view of the city below. Although he is happiest with both feet on shore, Percy likes to watch the boats and his old seafaring buddies coming into The Port.

PETE AND LILA

You've been glumped!

The problem with picnicking all the time is that you're particularly prone to cake-thieving predators like the ghastly Glump Bloopy!

Pete Slurp and Lila Tweet are the City's youngest picnicking duo. These little monsters are best buddies—you'll rarely see the chewing chums without each other. Their picnic basket is packed full of goopendous goodies, but their favorite munchies by far are Lila's mom's Quenut Butter sandwiches! Yum!

Monstrous hobbies

When she's not picnicking, talented Lila loves to sing. This budding monSTAR is the best singer at her school! Clawsomely-adventurous Pete collects rare slugs, builds stuff, and encourages Lila with her singing, despite being tone deaf!

DATA FILE
Hangout: Main Street
Catchphrases: "Nom, nom!"
Likes: Choir (Lila), Construction (Pete)
Often spotted: Mid-bite!

Two teeth are much better for munching than one!

Deceptively small mouth produces ear-shattering operatics!

PIP

DATA FILE
Moshling type: Nutties
Species: Savvy Sapling
Habitat: Wobbly Woods
Nuttie chums:
CocoLoco, Shelly

Playful Pip and the other sprightly Savvy Saplings are wild woodland Nutties, who are totally nuts about nature! Dressed in cute little acorn hats, these knowledgeable and curious critters get extremely excited about collecting berries, are obsessed with soil samples, and absolutely love leaping into piles of leaves!

Pip likes taking a little bit of green everywhere!

Hard hat to protect against falling chestnuts

Green Moshlings
These enthusiastic Moshlings really care about their surroundings, so they hate big-footed Moshling collectors who trample carelessly through their beautiful home.

Sturdy boots for climbing trees

A happy home
Savvy Saplings like Pip live either in Savvy Sapling Village, deep in the heart of the Wobbly Woods, or in little hidey-holes high up in the trees, hidden from view. Happiest surrounded by nature, Savvy Saplings like to play golf with twig clubs and mini gooberry balls, collect chestnuts, or listen to raindrops to help them relax.

Glump

Pirate Pong is most definitely the stinkiest Glump in all of Monstro City—and that's monstrously impressive, because Dr. Strangeglove's evil minions are all pretty smelly! Using his Stinky Winky Squint move as a secret weapon, Pong has everyone running away, holding their noses faster than they can say, "Peeew!"

Glump tower

Out on an evil mission for Dr. Strangeglove, the silly Glumps have bounced up the pirate ship's ladder and are now on top of each other in a precarious pile! Pirate Pong makes sure he'll be first on deck to investigate!

Eye patch stolen from a pirate

DATA FILE
Location: Top Secret
Job: Member of C.L.O.N.C.
Features: Pirate eye patch, pale, very smelly

Pong gives everyone the stink eye.

Perfecting the pong

Pong smells like a stinky pirate and with his evil eye patch, he looks like one too, hence the name! Eau de Pirate Pong smells like festering fish and steaming hot garbage, so steer clear of this reeking Glump at all times!

Skin is as white as a rattling old skull-and-crossbones.

141

PLINKY

Gleeful Plinky and the Squeezy TinkleHuffs love waltzing along the streets of Monstro City and tapping their toes in time to their tinkling tunes! These bold and bellowing accordion Moshlings originally come from Hurdy Gurdytown, but you'll often see them busking (and breathless) in Polka Park too.

DATA FILE
Moshling type: Tunies
Species: Squeezy TinkleHuff
Habitat: Hurdy Gurdytown and Polka Park
Tunie teammates: Wallop, Oompah, HipHop

Ticklish keyboard

Pushing the right buttons
A puffing TinkleHuff's keys are very ticklish. Its buttons are super sensitive, too: if you push them, it will hiccup and play out of tune. The only things that will make these musical Moshlings unhappy is the sound of bagpipes or the feel of long dirty fingernails tapping their treble boards!

Very loud, bellowing belly!

Music to Moshi ears
Tunie Plinky has a great sense of rhythm and often dances merrily through the valleys, looking for someone to serenade!

Toe-tapping tootsies!

142

POCITO

Pocito and the rest of the wrestling-obsessed Mini Manglers come from a secret training camp in the giant haystacks of El Astico Ranch, called the Atomic Slambuster. These super-strong Sporties are masters of countless clawsome wrestling moves, including the Full-Nelson Fajita and Spinning Headlock—ouch!

All fired up!

Athletic Pocito is a very brave Mini Mangler Moshling, who loves entertaining and putting on a fighting performance, even if it means turning into a critter cannonball!

Fighting face

Mini Manglers are incredibly stretchy and flexible, helping them beat their opponents with ease. But underneath all their grappling garb and brawling bravado, these masked Moshlings are very secretive souls. In their time-outs, they often like to nibble on nachos for dueling fuel and to cover themselves in talcum powder.

Mini Moshling muscles!

DATA FILE
Moshling type: Sporties
Species: Mini Mangler
Habitat: The Atomic Slambuster
Sportie sidekick: Rooby

Large mouth for grunting

Studded belt adds a bit of battle bling!

PODGE

Boing! Podge pounds the streets of Monstro City looking for Moshlings to lick up, quite literally! This Glump likes nothing better than using his long and twisty, sticky tongue as a large Lumpy Lasso to snap up unsuspecting Moshling victims. Poor little licked critters!

Bouncing ball
When he's on a monstrous mission, Podge bounces along like a super-fast bouncy ball. Watch out if you happen to be in this nasty Glump's perilous path!

Thick skin is great for bouncing on tough surfaces!

DATA FILE
Location: Top Secret
Job: C.L.O.N.C. minion
Features: Round, red, and podgy, with a smaller-than-average Glump mouth

Tongue is hidden, but ready to strike!

Fiendish features
Rounding up Moshlings like a cowboy is sour-faced Podge's favorite pastime. But in his rare spare time he likes perfecting his criminal C.L.O.N.C. look by using gloopy hair gel to spike his orange hair.

POOKY

The Potty Pipsqueak

DATA FILE

Moshling type: Dinos
Species: Potty Pipsqueak
Habitat: Make-Believe Valley
Dino playmates:
Doris, Gurgle, Snookums

Potty Pipsqueaks like Pooky originate from Make-Believe Valley. Sometimes they can also be seen inside spaceships, fire trucks, and tanks—but only ones that are made from cardboard boxes! Pipsqueaks say they wear eggshell helmets to shield themselves from Killer Canary attacks, but you can't always trust these Dinos to tell the truth!

Eggshell helmets make Pipsqueaks look like newly hatched Moshlings, or spacemen, or racing drivers!

Big head contains a huge imagination.

It's playtime!

These playful creatures love Jurassic Bark and acting out their favorite scenes with action figures. Often they're too busy playing to wash their paws before dinner. And then the silly squeaking Dinos like to play with their food too—they will only eat sausages if the skins are removed first. Fussy fossils!

Out of this world!

Like all Potty Pipsqueaks, incredibly imaginative Pooky loves make-believe and often pretends to be an amazing astronaut, zooming off in an imaginary spaceship to explore the swooniverse!

Cute button nose

POPPET

Loveable, huggalicious Poppets
appear to be timid tots who hate attention,
but when nobody can see them, they release their
inner boogie! Underneath their shy exterior, these
little cuties love nothing more than making music
and strutting their furry stuff on the dance floor!

Poppet party
Poppets love dressing up in
cute costumes and partying.
But when it comes to Halloween,
they find it really hard to
look scary—they're just
too adorable!

DATA FILE
Habitat: Monstro City
(and anywhere in the Moshi World)

Poppet phrases:
"Aww, shucks!",
"Let's boogie!",
"Quit staring!"

Monster mates:
Diavlo, Furi, Katsuma,
Luvli, Zommer

Cute, bashful
expression

Musical Moshis
"I ♥ Moshlings"
is Poppet's popilicious
pop song on the *Music
Rox* album. The video
features a Poppet who
loves Moshlings so much
she wants to attract as many
of the little critters as
possible—so sweet!

Pink is a Poppet's
favorite color.

Boots made
for bopping

Tickly Pickles like Prickles are particularly prickly and terribly ticklish pot-bound Moshlings. These scratchy, spiky critters love sitting on windowsills and puttering about in Itchypoo Park. Needless to say, you should think twice about approaching any of these irritated, itchy creatures!

Sneezing fit

When Ticklies scratch themselves (an occupational hazard for a Pickle), they sneeze. This fires enormous clouds of itching powder over themselves, making them. . . ahh . . . ahh. . . CHOO!

DATA FILE

Moshling type: Undiscovered
Species: Tickly Pickle
Habitat: Itchypoo Park
Likes: Satisfying scratching sessions

Beware these thorny spines!

Prickly pastimes

Tickly Pickles love to soothe their itching by soaking up rain and scratching one another's backs. However, they can't stand Sillipedes wriggling in their way or wobbly pots that threaten to make them topple over! A fall would be sure to lead to a sneezing attack!

Sturdy pot for balancing on the edges of windowsills

PRISCILLA

With their sparkling tiaras and graceful trotting technique, precious Princess Ponies like Priscilla are thought to have a majestic horsey heritage, despite coming from the humble area of Old Knackersville! They preen themselves, royal-wave with their hooves, and practice pirouettes for admiring audiences!

DATA FILE
Moshling type: Ponies
Species: Princess Ponie
Habitat: Old Knackersville
Ponie pals: Angel, Gigi, Mr. Snoodle

Shimmering crown

Magical mane (made with real horse hair!)

Haughty horses

Princess Ponies love the finer things in life, such as chomping on sparkly candy apples. They also spend a lot of time bragging about their winners' ribbons. These posh-looking ponies wouldn't be caught dead in frumpy flat shoes, as they're always trying to impress.

What a performance!

Like all Princess Ponies, Priscilla is a talented little trotter. These fancy fillies can make the hair on their manes and tails change color by tinkling their necklaces!

Her majesty's hooves (not made for hoovering!)

148

PROF. PURPLEX

The Owl of Wiseness

Well-read hoot-hooter

With Prof. Purplex's ravenous reading habits, swirling eyes are an owl-cupational hazard! Well, wouldn't reading an entire encyclopedia in a few seconds get your eyes spinning?!

Prof. Purplex and fellow outstandingly intellectual Owls of Wiseness are the brainiest birds in Birdie-dom! With their beaks burrowed in books, these tweeting nerdy birdies don't like to be interrupted. In fact, they will only leave the comfort of their tree branches if they ever run out of things to read.

All-seeing, all-reading eyes

DATA FILE
Moshling type: Birdies
Species: Owl of Wiseness
Habitat: High in the trees of Wobbly Woods
Birdie buddies: DJ Quack, Peppy, Tiki

Brainy birdies

Owls of Wiseness have no patience for stupidity. Unfortunately, these fact-finding feathery ones are no longer allowed in any libraries or bookshops... because they actually eat every single book and newspaper they read!

Sharp beak for gobbling pages

The Tubby Huggishi

PURDY

You'll find Purdy and the Tubby Huggishis lazing and lounging about in OuchiPoo Park. After feasting on paw-loads of pastry as well as chocolate, strawberry, and lemon ice scream, these huggable meowing Moshlings like to let their (larger than average) furry bellies hang out.

Kitty cakes
Like all Huggishis, goopendously greedy pussycat Purdy enjoys wolfing down monstrous amounts of purr-fectly iced cakes at teatime.

DATA FILE
Moshling type: Kitties
Species: Tubby Huggishi
Habitat: OuchiPoo Park near the Candy Cane Caverns in Sleepy Valley
Kittie chums: Gingersnap, Waldo, Lady Meowford

Full-fat diet
When not lapping up condensed milk or dipping their paws in syrup, Tubbies also love licking stamps. Perhaps they think stamps are food! The only exercise Tubbies are likely to get is from preening their Kittie fur or running (slowly) away from water pistols, which they hate!

Well-groomed fur

Round body, perfect for Huggishi hugs!

Paws for preening, buried deep within all that fur!

PU██-Fℇ--TION

Poor Purr-Fection was left behind at Hictoria Station and ended up in the Lost and Found! Luckily, some school-monsters were traveling through the station on their way to the Moshi Fun Park. When they saw him, they literally let the cat out of the bag, and took him back to their school with them!

The cat's meow
Lazing and lounging around on the school wall, Purr-Fection doesn't like to move too much. If you stroke him he might just about muster the energy to yawn and stretch!

Teachers' pet
After a fur-raising experience on the raaarghllercoaster rides at the Moshi Fun Park, Purr-Fection is now treated to a luxurious life in the school gardens. His Furriness is now fangtastically spoiled by all the children—and the teachers!

DATA FILE
Hangout: Ooh La Lane
Likes: Being fed, stroked, and generally spoiled!
Often spotted: Snoozing!

The sleepy cat's eyes rarely open.

Mouth wide for dribbling and drooling

Tail is scruffy after being caught in a suitcase.

151

Video Games Expert

Beaming down from a mysterious world somewhere deep in outer Moshi space, computer expert Raarghly has quickly become Monstro City's highest-scoring gaming geek. With the ability —and the hands—to play six games all at once, this two-toothed monster is Monstro City's ultimate unbeatable video-game champion!

Goggle eyes
With his big beady eyes, Raarghly does a great job of watching over the Games Starcade—while still playing plenty of video games himself, of course!

DATA FILE
Hangout: Games Starcade on Sludge Street
Catchphrase: "Game over!"
Likes: Err, gaming! What else is there?

Precise arm action

Out-of-this-world cuisine
Raarghly loves all sorts of space food and is particularly partial to monstrously tasty dehydrated ice cream. If you get your paws on any, make sure you feed it to him fast, and he'll soon be your "BAFF" (Best Alien Friend Forever)!

State-of-the-art spacecraft seat

Finger always on the button

RATTY

DATA FILE

Hangout: Dark corners of town
Likes: Monkey business
Catchphrase: Nothing.
He can't speak!
Often spotted:
Looking shifty

Monsterifically mischievous Ratty is constantly up to his naughty neck in no-good with his best pal Bug. They love playing practical jokes on everyone left, right, and Monstro City center. Watch out, because this dastardly duo is known to steal monstrous amounts of "souvenirs" everywhere they go.

Three eyes—all the better for seeing double (or triple) the trouble!

Hide and squeak!

Rascally rodent Ratty is often spotted (well, he is bright purple!) hiding behind things, ready to jump out and be a nuisance.

Shady shenanigans

Keeping three eyes out for potential tomfoolery, Ratty couldn't give a long, striped rat's tail if he's in trouble. When he's not with Bug, Ratty enjoys hanging out with his only other friend, the Dodgy Dealer —doing dodgy stuff, no doubt!

Ratty loves putting his paws in everyone's business.

His ratty old "tattle-tail" always gives him away.

153

RICKETY BOO

Roarker Rickety Boo is a bit of a busybody. He wields his road sign at any Moshi who passes, demanding them to "STOP!" in their monster tracks. There's a rumor flying around Monstro City that Rickety was actually fired some time ago for being so bossy, but he just can't find a better way to spend his days, so he continues to work!

DATA FILE

Catchphrase: "Everything's Rickety Boo!"

Likes: Getting in the way, eating moldy bread off his head

Often spotted: Bringing the City to a standstill

Rickety is always carrying his stop sign.

Hold up!

Boo! With just a raise of his paw, Rickety has the power (and the huge red stop sign) to jump out and cause gridlock chaos on the streets of Monstro City.

Munching on the move

Rickety stores half-eaten sandwiches under his hard hat so he can chomp on them when he gets tired of holding up the same old sign, stacking cones, and other boring but roadworthy tasks. Rickety's absolute favorite sandwich is smelly jelly and crab. What a clawsome flavor combination!

Rickety stands all day, so he makes sure he wears sturdy, but comfortable boots.

ROARY SCRAWL

DATA FILE

Hangout: *The Daily Growl* office

Likes: Eavesdropping, collecting ABC (already-been-chewed) gumballs

Often spotted: Monster-watching across the City

Roving reporter Roary Scrawl keeps his many eyes out for the next big story to print in *The Daily Growl*, Monstro City's goopendous newspaper. Editor-in-chief Roary loves tap-tapping away on his typewriter as fast as monsterly possible, keeping the City up-to-date with his super-informative ooze bulletins.

Easy on the eyes

Romantic Roary's favorite holiday is Valentine's Day, and he only has eyes for his gorgeous girlfriend Tyra Fangs. They enjoy building sandcastles at Bleurgh Beach and going on romantic candlelit dinner dates. But if Eye Pie is on the menu, the night will be ruined because squeamish Scrawl will totally freak out!

Roary is a dapper dude. He always wears a smart yellow bow tie.

Editor-in-chief Roary keeps an eye on everything!

Eye-spy eyes

Because Roary has eyes in the back of his head (and the front and sides for that matter!), he is a monstrous multitasker. He can look for his misplaced eyeballs, even when he's busy working on a story!

155

ROCKO

Grumpy Glumpy Rocko hates everything and everyone, even the other Glumps! Preferring to keep himself to himself, Dr. Strangeglove's nasty minion is often spotted wobbling around Monstro City on his own. But Moshlings, beware! Rocko may be alone, but he knows how to give a mean "Rocko Blocko Backroll!"

DATA FILE
Location: Top Secret
Job: C.L.O.N.C. minion
Features: Angry, aggressive, solitary

Scary snaggle-tooth

Aggressive glare

Lonesome Glump
Rocko is very unfriendly and a total loner. He rarely speaks, but that's no loss because no Moshi would want to speak to this gloomy Glump anyway!

Rotten Rocko
Everything about revolting Rocko is negative and unhappy! His eyebrows are set in a constant frown and he never, ever smiles. Maybe he just needs some new friends to cheer him up?

DATA FILE

Moshling type: Worldies
Species: Baby Blockhead
Habitat: Beaster Island
Worldie chums:
Liberty, Cleo, Mini Ben

Baby Blockheads like Rocky may look stone-faced, but they are always willing to lend a very strong helping hand. When they're not sweating liquid concrete from lifting heavy objects, they sit for hours and hours, just gazing at Potion Ocean. These heavy-weight hunks of rock can be a little dense!

Bulging eyes stare out to sea.

Solid as a rock

Rocky and his Blockhead buddies don't realize their own strength, so they end up breaking things by accident. Monsters should watch their fingers when they shake hands with a Blockhead! But these hard-to-the-core Worldies do have a softer side too, as they love fluffy-wuffy rabbits!

Blockheads are always cracking up!

Rocking out!

With a name like Rocky, it's not surprising to hear that the baby boulder absolutely loves rock music. This tough dude sure knows how to beat those drums, hard!

ROFL

Jabbering Jibberlings like Rofl are lively little chattering critters. They hurry and scurry around, babbling about utter gibberish. Unfortunately, once these manic Moshlings are wound up, there is very little chance of stopping them! The only thing that works is drenching them in soup gloop. This stops them... eventually!

Clipper critter

Rofl is a handy Smilie who can be used as monster hair clippers. When gooperstar Zack Binspin's mane nearly engulfed him on a Super Moshi mission, little Rofl saved him from a hairy situation!

Cheesy grin

Nattering nonsense

Jolly Jabbering Jibberlings jibber-jabber jauntily with their jet-fast jaws! Now say that twenty times! A Jibberling could, as they practice tongue-twisting all day long! When they're not chattering or smiling, they like gnashing corn on the cob, despite getting the little bits stuck in their teeth.

Twist the cog to start the jabbering!

DATA FILE

Moshling type: Smilies
Species: Jabbering Jibberling
Habitat: Mouthy Hollow and Music Island
Smilie sidekick: Tiamo

ROLAND JONES

Roland Jones spends most of his time drinking ultra-bubbly wobble-ade at The Port. You might think he's just very thirsty, but in fact Roland hopes that the bubbly stuff will help him to grow to be the same size as his siblings, who are more than twice as big as he is!

Roly-poly Roland

Mr. Jones buys a bottle of wobble-ade every 15 minutes! After a day of glugging the foamy stuff, Roland can be spotted wobbling from side to side and rolling all the way home!

Large mouth for guzzling

DATA FILE
Hangout: The Port
Catchphrase: "Glug, glug, glug!"
Likes: Collecting empty wobble-ade bottles

Glazed, unfocused eyes due to drinking too much wobble-ade

Pop!

Roland doesn't appear to be getting any taller, just full of air! With wobble-ade sloshing around his tummy, this furry ball of bubbles is constantly hiccupping, burping, and having monstrous bodily-function issues! Gross!

Trying desperately to keep his balance

ROOBY

Look out for Plucky Puncharoos, who hail from the faraway land of Downunder and recently hopped to Monstro City. Residents are warned to avoid straying into a Puncharoo's path, because gutsy Roos like Rooby will do anything to protect the pals in their pouches—even though they're actually just stuffed animals!

Looking for a fight?
Plucky Puncharoos are always looking to perfect their technique. Furis make great sparring partners for some paw-swinging practice!

DATA FILE:

Moshling type: Sporties

Species: Plucky Puncharoo

Habitat: Downunder

Sportie sidekick: Pocito

Long nose for sniffing out potential threats

Big shiny red boxing gloves

The cute little toy in the Puncharoo's pouch is stuffed with jelly beans!

Puncharoo playtime
These bouncing beauties love flinging a sausage on the barbecue and playing with boomerangs over and over again. This doesn't leave much time for watching daytime soap operas, but Rooby and the other Roos would never watch them anyway—they can't stand them!

ROXY

Great getaway

Prisms may be more than a little bit brittle, but they are very quick on their dainty feet. When chased by enthusiastic Moshling Collector Buster Bumblechops, Roxy can easily give him a run for his money!

Precious Prisms like Roxy are priceless gems and secretive souls. They are very particular, and wear white gloves, so they don't mark or smudge anything—especially their own very valuable selves! Prisms are extremely fussy, which makes sense when you realize that they could shatter into tiny pieces at any moment!

Shiny, spotless surface

Fragile face:
DO NOT TOUCH!

Squeaky clean

These delightfully delicate gems love lounging in luxurious vinegar baths and buffing themselves on polishing machines until they gleam. They absolutely loathe shiny-object-stealing magpies, and spotting fuzzy fingerprints.

Pristine clean white gloves worn for protection

DATA FILE
Moshling type: Secrets
Species: Precious Prism
Habitat: Top Secret
Secret friend: Blingo

ROY G. BIV

Vividly bright Roy G. Biv is a multicolored monster and professional Rainbow Rider, who takes his name from the first letter of each of the colors of the rainbow. This totally rad hero is also Monstro City's connoisseur on Colossal Cloud Cruising and the authority on all things bright and colorful.

Roy G. Biv Day

Magical Roy only comes to Monstro City once a year on what has become known as Roy G. Biv Day. He spends the day making sure that there will be rainbows all year round.

Bright idea

Rainbow master Roy likes to blend in with his surroundings by sporting as many colors as monstrously possible! He dyes his hair green, has bright blue skin, and regularly dips his horns in rainbow paint to keep them looking nice and stripy. Well, this technicolor whizz has got to look the part!

Caped cloud crusader!

DATA FILE

Hangout: The skies

Catchphrase: "That's, like, totally colorful, dude!"

Likes: Sky surfing, riding rainbows, going to Colossal Cloud Cruising conventions

Spotted: Once a year above Monstro City

Bright sun-yellow tummy

Strong tail used for balance while sky surfing

RUBY SCRIBBLEZ

DATA FILE

Hangout: Wherever Zack Binspin is (or as nearby as possible)

Catchphrase: "Write your way to the top!"

Likes: Shopping for new trends, bargain hunting

Often spotted: Scribbling away

Friendly but pushy Ruby Scribblez began her career writing dull labels for Yukea, the furniture store. Luckily, she soon climbed the wobbly work ladder to become a roving reporter for *Shrillboard Magazine*, the author of many monsterific celebrity biographies, and a top-rated talk show host.

Scruffy, trendy tresses

Star-struck eyes

Monstrous ambition

Miss Scribblez writes a clawsome blog, *Ruby's Review* for *The Daily Growl*, in which she reviews all the latest games and toys. She also created the fanzine for the band Hairosniff and is rumored to have dated the group's lead singer, Screech McPiehole.

Binspin's got her head spinning!

Ruby simply adores pop solo gooperstar Zack Binspin. She will find any excuse to interview him and stare longingly into his starry eyes!

Big mouth for all that gossiping and interviewing

SCAMP

Scamp and the rest of the Froggie Doggie pack are dogs who think they are frogs! Dressed in frog costumes, the funny Puppies swap a dog's life for pond life and barking for ribbitting. These deluded Doggies are happiest boinging along and dreaming about fairy princesses, however confusing it may seem to everyone else!

DATA FILE
Moshling type: Puppies
Species: Froggie Doggie
Habitat: Lillypad Lake and Croak Creek
Puppie pals:
Fifi, McNulty, White Fang

Inflatable Froggie fancy dress

Up the creek!
Scamp likes to go to Lillypad Lake and Croak Creek, but the loopy-loo pooch can't actually swim—not even doggie paddle! Fortunately, Babs is there to give the daft Doggie a row in her boat.

Pop goes the Frog!
The best way to get your paws on one of these happy hounds is by tugging on their pretty pink bows. This will make their rubbery Froggie outfit deflate! You can also make these Puppies' costumes pop with a pin. So, the Froggie Doggies are somewhat scared of knitting needles!

Bow secures froggie costume.

The nearest Froggie Doggies get to barking is being barking mad!

SCARLET O'HAIRA

Loving and loveable Scarlet O'Haira and fellow flaming-red Fluffy Snugglers are easy to spot, but it's a complete Moshling mystery as to where the cuddly critters come from. These friendly balls of fluff are happy huggers, who just want to turn every Moshi's frown upside down!

All snuggled up!

Quite frankly my Moshi dears, Scarlet O'Haira doesn't give a gooberry about anything other than cozying up with fellow Fluffy Snugglers. Cute!

Extra soft and furry, for your cuddling comfort!

DATA FILE

Moshling type: Mythies
Species: Fluffy Snuggler
Habitat: No Moshi knows
Mythie mates: Shambles, Long Beard, Jessie

Warm and fuzzies

Affectionate Fluffy Snugglers will hug everyone and everything, whether they like it or not! These Mythies will even give lampposts and trees a squeeze! You may also find these extremely warm-spirited fuzzy furballs cheering you on—using their fluffy selves as pompoms, of course!

Arms out, ready for a warm embrace!

165

SCRUMPY

Surreal Snoopers like Scrumpy fulfill their curious natures by sneaking around the Moshi world, poking and prying into everyone's business! These nosey parkers and their sensitive snozzles are based in and around Strudel Station, but are often found out and about investigating mysteries.

DATA FILE
Moshling type: Arties
Species: Surreal Snooper
Habitat: Strudel Station
Often spotted: Running away from apple-munching Ponies

No proper detective should be without a moustache.

Hat is an attempt to disguise appleness while out sleuthing.

One of a kind
When they're not out sleuthing, Surreal Snoopers are utterly odd and exceedingly surreal! The creative critters love the smell of oil and paint. If that isn't strange enough, they ride around on pasta unicycles, and are often seen wearing meat shoes on their heads and wrapping fish around their waists!

Soft soles for quiet snooping

Inspector Scrumpy
Scrumpy thinks his moustache and hat make the perfect disguise. In fact, the odd-looking Moshling looks incredibly conspicuous as he wanders the streets of Monstro City!

SHAMBLES

Spirited Shambles and the rest of the happy Scrappy Chappy crew like to chill out high up in the trees of Wingledeed Woods. These messy Mythies are very content to look scruffy, so you'll never see them sporting an elegant necktie or styling their fur to look good.

Shrubbery somersaults

Shambles loves extreme hedge diving with fellow furballs! This is probably why this Scrappy Chappy, and all the other muddled critters, always look like they've been dragged through the bushes backward—literally!

Gnawed ear

Scruffy feathers never see styling gel.

DATA FILE
Moshling type: Mythies
Species: Scrappy Chappy
Habitat: Wingledeed Woods
Mythie pals:
Jessie, Long Beard,
Scarlet O'Haira

Self-snacking
Scrappy Chappies have the yucky habit of nibbling on their own ears, which they claim taste particularly yummy dunked in pucumber dip! Luckily for them, their ears grow back, so they always have a never-ending supply of earsnax!

Scrappy flappy hands are surprisingly strong for tearing through bushes.

SHELBY

Shelby and the other Slapstick Tortoises are Ninja Moshlings. When they're not hibernating under the boardwalk at Groan Bay, they head to the Wailing Wharf to compare their clumsy combat moves. However, their intensive Ninja training seems to have failed them, as these gawky creatures always end up belly-side up!

Tortoise on gloop

Shelby loves gloop-skating, despite finding it hard to stay upright in the icky stuff. Clumsy Shelby often ends up covered in gloop!

Hopeless hardshells

These crazy critters are pretty useless, wasting their time doing things like brushing their teeth with toffee! Their idea of Ninja training is watching kung fu movies rather than actually practicing the moves—they haven't even learned how to tie their own Ninja bandanas!

Bandana, tied by a friend

Slapstick Tortoises' shells may get scratched, but they always look perfectly buffed.

DATA FILE

Moshling type: Ninjas

Species: Slapstick Tortoise

Habitat: Groan Bay and the Wailing Wharf

Ninja pals: Sooki-Yaki, Chop Chop, General Fuzuki

SHELLY

The Nattering Nutling

DATA FILE
Moshling type: Nutties
Species: Nattering Nutling
Habitat: Goober Gulch
Nuttie chums:
CocoLoco, Pip

Super-chatty Shelly and the other Nattering Nutlings can often be spotted gossiping in Goober Gulch. These chitchatting critters enjoy long discussions about incredibly important matters, such as super monSTAR-sightings, who is dating who, and which Moshi is wearing what!

Wide-eyed with excitement

Cute bow fit for a gooperstar

Loose lips!

MonSTARs in their eyes
The scandal-hungry Nattering Nutlings are totally nuts about celebrities! With their over-excitable and inquisitive natures, they devote their time to swooning over the rich and famous and reading the latest Ruby Scribblez celebrity biographies.

Wannabe gooperstar!
Nattering Nutling Shelly likes to plaster the walls with pop posters. The Nuttie sings *Music Rox* album songs in front of the mirror, pretending to be Monstro City's hottest new gooperstar!

Even since she was but a squirt of a Splurt, bubbly and gooey Shelly has been the world record holder for holding her breath the longest. With her natural-born talents and a body made up of a sticky, bubbly substance, light-headed Shelly is always happily floating on air—or in icky slime!

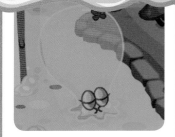

Forever blowing bubbles
Shelly is very skilled at holding her breath and blowing herself up into a big bubbly balloon, completely changing her shape. It's pretty Splurt-tastic to watch!

DATA FILE
Hangout:
The Underground Tunnels
Catchphrase:
"Take a breath!"
Likes: Holding her breath and counting to 5,000!

Big, round bubble-shaped eyes!

Sticky bubble is full of hot air!

Airy fairy
Shelly Splurt loves inhaling and exhaling at The Underground Tunnels, where she's currently training to become an exsplurt blimp at next year's Monster Carnival. She's hoping to take everyone's breath away with her performance!

SHISHI

Sneezing Pandas like ShiShi are hopelessly hooked on Monstrovision. Watching the screen so much makes them very well informed, but it also makes them sneeze! In fact, their noses are constantly sniffly. Some say it must be an allergic reaction to Monstrovision, but no one knows for sure.

A big night in
ShiShi likes nothing better than snuggling up on the sofa in front of the box, with a big tub of wamwoo shoots to nibble on and an extra-large pack of super-soft tissues at the ready!

DATA FILE
Moshling type: Beasties
Species: Sneezing Panda
Habitat: Gogglebox Gulch
Beastie buddies: Jeepers, Burnie, Humphrey

Google-eyed critters
These Monstrovision-watching, channel-hopping Sneezies are happy to go anywhere there's a perfectly positioned seat in front of a big screen. When there's nothing good to watch, Sneezing Pandas busy themselves by scrunching up tissues, using refreshing eye drops and avoiding pepper!

Wide eyes for viewing Monstrovision

Tasty wamwoo shoots

Good paw reflexes for using remote controls

TE - EWMA

The Shrewman is a shaggy-furred, shy, and withdrawn soul who lives in a tree in the Wobbly Woods. Despite hiding himself away, he actually has a very kind and helpful nature. However, he's rarely spotted in Monstro City, as he's too timid to venture beyond the safety of the trees!

DATA FILE
Hangout: Up a tree
Catchphrase: "Tap, tap, tap!"
Likes: Writing books, eating berries
Sometimes spotted: Peeking out from his tree trunk

Trunk-brown fur acts as perfect critter camouflage.

Homely hideout
The timid Shrewman seldom strays from his comfortable tree trunk home. However, he is sometimes spotted through the leaves, stealing a quick but shrewd look at the outside world!

Speedy typewriter-tapping paws

Berry-tastic books
The Shrewman is a fussy eater, but he loves berries and even uses their juice as typewriter ink. This may be because he's too scared to go to the shops, but it clearly works—he's an award-winning author! This berry-powered writer is secretive, shy, and only sits down to type if he thinks no one can hear him!

SIMON GROWL

Blunt and grumpy Simon Growl is a fangtastic talent scout, but a mean judge; he likes to tell you exactly what he thinks—and even if he doesn't, his scary hair will show you how he really feels! Si lives in Growl Mansion, but spends most of his time in the studio, managing his record label HighPants Productions, and mingling with A-list celebs.

With hair like this, who needs friends?!

The face of a lean, mean judging machine!

The real talent?

Not-so-simple Simon has often claimed to be the real writer of the best-selling music in Monstro City, rather than the gooperstars themselves. Maybe his success is going to his head? Either way, Simon definitely isn't afraid to give himself the top score!

Probably the highest waistline in town

DATA FILE
Hangout: The Underground Disco
Catchphrase: "I'm an all-round genius."
Likes: Scowling and growling
Often spotted: Surrounded by paparazzi

Strike 1

Groaning Growl is by far the toughest judge on the panel at The Underground Disco. So you'd better watch your dance steps around him, or you'll be going home as fast as you can say, "5, 6, 7, 8!"

SKEETER RYDELL

Monsterifically hardworking Skeeter Rydell drives up and down Gift Island all hours of the day and night on his slow, unsteady shiny red scooter. He's the only deliveryman on the island, so he's always in a hurry. There's no time like the present!

Keeps his eyes peeled

Scooter in metallic Twistmas-present red

The bigger the box, the better the present!

Scooter search

As well as delivering presents, scootin' tootin' Skeeter combs the streets of Gift Island looking for his wife and their seven children. Apparently they made their home out of presents somewhere, and since then he hasn't been able to find them!

Wrap, ride, and go

Delivering gifts on the bustling, paper-rustling streets of Gift Island is a pretty big task, so as soon as Skeeter has reached a delivery destination, he has to Skeet-daddle to the next. He doesn't mind though, because his deliveries make lots of people happy.

SLY CHANCE

Dodgy Dealer

Sly Chance spent his somewhat shady mini-monster-hood on the beaches of The Shifty Shack Sandbar, munching on Quicksand-wiches. Little else is known about this crooked character's past, or how he became the dodgy dealer he is today, so most monsters should be suspicious of this devious dealer dude.

Wheeler Dealer!

Want to get rid of some stuff quickly? Head to Sly's Dodgy Dealz store on Sludge Street! But keep your wits about you—this tentacled trickster may try to pull the Furi wool over your eyes!

Sly keeps his cards close to his hat.

Sly wears the jewelery he has bought from monsters—at a bargain price, of course!

Where would shady Sly be without his shades?

DATA FILE

Hangout: Dodgy Dealz
Catchphrase: "I'll give you a good price, honest!"
Likes: Tapping his tentacles, dancing in the dark

A done deal

Monsters from all across Monstro City visit Sly's shop to sell unwanted items. When *The Daily Growl* editor Roary Scrawl took his prized Shakesfear bust to the dodgy dealer, he played his cards right and managed to win 90 percent of his Rox back! Shifty Sly must've been in a good mood that day!

175

SNOOKUMS

Ever since they hatched from marzipan eggs, sweet little Snookums and the other Baby Tumteedums have been searching for someone to take care of them. Despite their baby-blue appearance, these dinky Dinos are actually aging backward, so the littlest ones are already ancient!

DATA FILE

Moshling type: Dinos
Species: Baby Tumteedum
Habitat: Near a yuckberry bush or at Stinky Hollow
Dino playmates: Doris, Pooky, Gurgle

Dependent Dinos
Cuddly Baby Tumteedums are adorable. They love hanging with—and onto—everyone, including Buster Bumblechops. But sometimes their constant clinginess can be a little too much.

The cutest tongue in Monstro City

Adorable arms— ready for a hug!

Critter comforts
Cute little Snookums and the sensitive Tumteedums love their critter comforts, so they often wear comfy slippers. And if they hear loud music, they protect their tiny Tumteedum ears with their prehistoric paws!

Tumteedum tummies love a tickle or two.

SNOOZE CRUISE

Horizontally unchallenged, Snooze Cruise is undeniably the sleepiest monster in Monstro City. When he was just a little critter, Snooze was struck down after drinking a strange sleeping potion, which has meant he has spent a super-slumbering 92 percent of his life asleep!

If you snooze, you lose

Snooze can sleep on anything, anywhere, and next to anyone! He spends his whole life missing out on things, but with that big grin permanently on his face, he doesn't seem to mind!

All that sleeping can lead to RMEM—Rapid Monster Eye Movement.

DATA FILE
Hangout:
The Underground Tunnels
Catchphrase: "Zzzzzzzz!"
Likes: Dreaming, sleep-eating
Often spotted:
Monsternapping!

Dreaming happy dreams

Big cushioned head acts as a pillow.

Noisy napper
Dozey Snoozey snores so loudly that he keeps The Underground Tunnel bats away! When he's not snoring, Cruise spends his time daydreaming about soaking up siestas or catching forty (thousand) winks!

177

SNOZZLE WOBBLESON

Snozzle Wobbleson started out his career as a Stock Monster at the Gross-ery Store. But everything he picked up slipped through his wobbly grip and made a splat-tastic mess everywhere! Luckily, Snozzle was soon given the more suitable job of cashier, which he loves. Except when he has to handle jelly, that is!

DATA FILE
Hangout: Gross-ery Store
Catchphrase: "Snozzle stocks the lot!"
Likes: Wobbling contests, dodge ball
Often spotted: Snacking on Slopcorn

What a mess!
Snozzle doesn't like to think back to his messy time working in the stock room. He is much happier floating around the shop, serving all the hairy customers.

Wobbleson creations
Despite his busy day job, Snozzle still finds time to invent monsterific new treats to sell. He cleverly concocted his own drink, "Essence of Gloop," and in honor of Growly Grub Day, sold his latest creations, Curry and Saffron flavored Glump Cakes. Yum!

Jelly legs

Wobbly frame

SNUFFY HOOKUMS

DATA FILE

Hangout: The great Moshi outdoors
Catchphrase: "Moshling-tastic!"
Likes: Exploring, adventuring, collecting
Often spotted: Springing out of bushes

Snuffy Hookums is Buster Bumblechops' faithful sidekick and a leading expert in Moshlingology (that's all things Moshling to those not in the collectors' circle!). Snuffy once vanished on an intrepid Moshling mission near Mount KrakkaBlowa. Many assumed something monsterifically terrible had happened, but it turned out that she was just a bit lost.

Monstrous mullet hat!

The fur-fect disguise

Snuffy's super-furry Moshling-stalker's hat is great camouflage. It does a clawsome job of concealing her from critters as she studies them in their natural habitats.

Fangtastic findings

When heroic Ms. Hookums eventually made it back to Monstro City, she had many a Moshling tale to tell about her voyage of discovery. She collected critters, encountered a mysterious tribe, and had many fur-raising adventures!

A large rucksack packed with Moshlingologist essentials.

SOOKI-YAKI

Sleek Caped Assassins like Sooki-Yaki can sometimes be spotted clinging to drainpipes and squeezing through miniscule gaps. These swift assassins have the amazing ability to disappear and reappear in just an instant! Unfortunately, the risky kitties can't control their vanishing powers, so they always reappear when they shouldn't!

Awful escape artists
Caped Assassins are often caught suspended in midair, floating around in cat-astrophically visible positions!

DATA FILE

Moshling type: Ninjas

Species: Caped Assassin

Habitat: Last seen scaling a drainpipe near East Grumble

Ninja chums: Chop Chop, Shelby, General Fuzuki

Large bushy tail helps Sooki-Yaki balance when swinging from rooftop to rooftop.

Dark full-body catsuit for blending into the shadows

Leisure purr-suits

When they're not busy on Ninja adventures and tiptoeing dangerously along slippery rooftops, Sooki-Yaki and the other Caped Assassins like playing with the latest gadgets. They're also good at knitting clothes, but never collars, as they hate wearing ones that itch!

SPLUTNIK

Zoshling

DATA FILE
Habitat: Swooniverse
Job: Chief Engineer of the *Rhapsody 2*
Zoshling crew: Captain Squirk, First Officer Ooze, Dr. C. Fingz

Space-brained Splutnik is an energetic zooming Zoshling who can rocket-race across the Silky Way on his jet pack in less than 12 seconds. Zwhoosh! This fast-moving extraterrestrial is also quick-thinking, so he is well suited to his role as Chief Engineer on board the *Rhapsody 2*, the Zoshlings' high-tech spacecraft.

Enormous brain protected by helmet.

Missing in action
After the *Rhapsody 2* crashed, the Super Moshis found Splutnik at Bobbi SingSong's yoga retreat in Jollywood. Evil Big Chief Tiny Head had put Splutnik in a deep trance in order to steal his jet pack!

Trusty jet pack

Intergalactic genius
Famous for being the Zoshling who discovered the Bossanova Goopernova when he was just a young space cadet, Splutnik has always been a super space geek. When he's not dazzling his alien pals with his cosmic intelligence, he likes to relax by playing the kazoo.

Holding on very tightly!

SPROCKETT

Sprockett is a serious and soulless robot, with a super short fuse! He and his hyperactive partner Hubbs make up S&H Industries, the accident-prone creators of many of C.L.O.N.C.'s most wicked weapons and contraptions. They even built a Super Weapon to destroy the sun. But Sprockett didn't care—as long as he met the deadline!

DATA FILE

Often spotted: In the Top Secret C.L.O.N.C. Laboratory

Catchphrase: "Bleep, bleep, brink!"

Likes: Tinkering with stuff, breaking things

Brain processor the size of a shriveled splatsuma!

Single blinking eye

Monster mistake

Sprockett thinks that he is the brainy half of S&H Industries, but this seems unlikely considering the teeny-weeny size of his central processor! In fact, both daft robots were sacked by C.L.O.N.C. because they didn't notice that the Super Moshis had sabotaged their designs for the Super Weapon, causing it to malfunction!

Boggy blunder!

Sprockett and Hubbs faced a squelchy ordeal when they fell into the Snaggletooth Swamp. Silly Sprockett got them gloopendously lost in the jungle, after they were both fired by C.L.O.N.C.

Heart made of cogs

SQUIDGE

Squealing Squidge and the rest of the Furry Heebee flock are creepy critters who hang out (upside down) in the Crazy Caves of Fang-Ten Valley. It's unusual to spot these diabolical bloodsucking beings, as they only fly around at night, looking for things to bite. But if you do see a bat-winged Spookie, it'll definitely give you the Heebee-jeebies!

Fang attack!
Dun-dun-dun! Furry Heebees like Squidge love to make a spine-chillingly dramatic entrance, by swooping down with fangs and claws exposed, ready for some neck nipping!

Scary-wary hair

DATA FILE
Moshling type: Spookies
Species: Furry Heebee
Habitat: Crazy Caves of Fang-Ten Valley
Spookie chums: Big Bad Bill, Ecto, Kissy

Wicked monster wings

Biting beasts
When there aren't any necks to nibble, Heebees enjoy a cup of instant tomato soup with lots of garlic croutons instead. In their spare time, these hairy Spookies like wearing long capes, listening to hair-raising organ music, and avoiding Heebee Repellent Spray!

Mouth wide open for high-pitched screeching

183

SQUIFF

DATA FILE
Location: Top Secret
Job: C.L.O.N.C. minion
Features: Golden, silly, and smelly!

Funny-featured Squiff looks harmless, with his three eyes, buck teeth, and silly hair, but he's actually Dr. Strangeglove's secret weapon of mass foul-smelling inhalation! That's because this naughty golden nugget has ferocious flatulence power and lets rip with putrid Squiff Stinkbombs! Foul play indeed!

Three eyes—all of different sizes

Squiff's coif!

Stinkbomb ahoy!
With his mouth gaping open and dripping with drool, Glump Squiff propels himself along with his fetid flatulence!

Reeking rascal
Talented Squiff has the ability to break wind on Dr. Strangeglove's command. It is rumored that the gases from these lethal Stinkbombs are trapped and used to keep the C.L.O.N.C. blimp afloat!

STACEY GRACE

Sweet little schoolgirl Stacey goes to the goopendously renowned Miss Jingle's School for Girls. This clumsy little critter struggles to tie her shoelaces and often stumbles and falls over as a result! Luckily, her mom is very understanding, and lets her go to school in her bare feet instead.

Waiting game
Stacey Grace can often be found sitting on the bridge at The Port, waiting patiently for her friends from school. Sometimes she's waiting a long time....

Listening out for her gossipy school gal pals

Girly greetings
Cute as a monstrously purple button, girly Stacey Grace enjoys waving and smiling her two-toothed grin at any Moshi who passes by. She also spends a lot of time hiding her feet so that no one can stamp on her little, shoeless plum-colored toes as they walk by!

DATA FILE
Hangout: The Port
Catchphrase: "Oops!"
Likes: I-Spy, playing on the bridge
Often Spotted: Stepping in yucky things with her bare feet!

Sociable Stacey loves waving her paw at other critters.

185

STANLEY

Songful SeaHorses like Stanley can be annoyingly noisy, as they like to whistle utterly terrible show tunes all day long! These crooning critters are often found bobbing up and down in Reggae Reef's shallow waters. But despite their obviously fishy nature, the Songful SeaHorses can't actually swim very well!

Whistle while you bathe!
Stanley loves whistling in the safe shallow water of the bath, but never uses bubble bath. After all, what's the point when the SeaHorses can blow their own bubbles?

DATA FILE
Moshling type: Fishies
Species: Songful SeaHorse
Hangout: Reggae Reef
Fishie friends:
Blurp, Fumble, Cali

Songful SeaHorses love listening to kazoo concertos.

Razzmatazz!
These flamboyant musical Fishies love to put on a show. To add to the whole silly Songful spectacle, every ear-splitting tune they whistle is accompanied by lots of bubbles and ridiculous dancing. Some say this is to attract fellow SeaHorses, but no one has hung around long enough to find out!

Long nose blows the best bubbles in town.

Lips poised for an irritating whistling session!

STASHLEY SNOOZER

It may seem like Stashley Snoozer is always fast asleep, but he's actually keeping track of things with his furry hat! With four eyes in the front of his curious cap, Stashley is totally aware of everything that's happening on Main Street. Naughty monsters, watch out!

On guard!
Stashley is very well groomed, except for the scruffy hair on his hat! When he's awake he stands to attention, but it's hard to take Stashley seriously with his hilarious handlebar moustache.

All-seeing hat

Efficient snoozing
Stashley Snoozer is the greatest multitasking monster in all of Monstro City. He slouches on his stool, puts his paws up, and catches 40 winks. Despite this, he is still able to keep an eye out for trouble on Main Street, thanks to his hat.

DATA FILE
Hangout: Main Street

Catchphrase:
"Eye can spy you!"

Hobbies:
Snoring, polishing boots, ironing his uniform

Often spotted:
Almost falling off his stool

Stashley keeps his moustache nicely waxed.

The baton is just for show; it's actually made of soft rubber!

187

SUEY

Bashful Bowlheads like Suey are made in Won Ton Bay on Hong Bong Island. These shy dishes of the day have bowl-shaped heads that hold never-ending supplies of oodles of noodles! Just don't try to use a Bowlhead's chopsticks to eat the noodles, as they're actually delicate feelers that they use to sense danger.

DATA FILE
Moshling type: Munchies
Species: Bashful Bowlhead
Habitat: Won Ton Bay
Munchie friend:
Fizzy

Noodles never run out, so dig in!

Chopstick-like feelers

Fortune favors the bowls
Like all Bashful Bowlheads, Suey is very timid and finds it hard to make friends. But she believes in destiny, and feels that fate brought her together with Tingaling and the other Kittens of Good Fortune.

Tangy taste
Hot and spicy Bowlheads love five-spice chips and flavorful fortune cookies, which they search for in the Terry Aargh Keys. These chopsticky chums can't stand it if pointy cutlery comes too close, though, and they're petrified of lemon dishwasher soap ruining their noodles' fiery flavor.

A little body for such a big bowl head!

SWEET TOOTH

Sweet Tooth is a nasty piece of dental work, and as rotten as a cavitied tooth! This sugary rascal is a member of the criminal group C.L.O.N.C. and is armed up to the gums with a Hypno Blaster Lollipop, Cavity Candy Bombs, Kaleido Beams, and Lolly Lasers! Sweet Moshi, those weapons sound scarily scrumptious!

Candy Cane Caves

Sweet Tooth practices using criminal loads of weapons in this delicious lair. The villain's weapon of choice is the Hypno Blaster Lollipop. Wise Elder Furi and Buster Bumblechops are immune to its hypnotic effects, but other monsters can try to fight it by making the sound of a dentist's drill!

Hypno Blaster Lollipop—you are feeling sugary, very sugary!

Wig made from cotton candy. Sweet Tooth saves a honeycomb and desiccated coconut wig for special occasions.

Sweet by name, NOT by nature

Nobody knows if Sweet Tooth is a he or a she, and it's best not to ask, as the last monster who did ended up in the moshpital! In fact, Sweet Tooth is so frostingly frightening, Simon Growl was too scared to invite the evil one to his studio to record the song Sweet Tooth Stomp, so it was made in the Candy Cane Caves!

Sweet Tooth's drool is actually Pure Evil Treacle, a result of eating too much candy!

DATA FILE:

Habitat: Unknown

Catchphrase: "Sweet Tooth Stomp!"

Likes: Counting sweets in jars, scary singing

Always spotted: Drooling

TAMARA TESLA

DATA FILE
Hangout: The Observatory
Catchphrase: "Greetings!"
Likes: Watching weird Monstrovision, science conventions
Often spotted: Thinking hard!

Tamara Tesla is totally and utterly monsterifically bright! Born out of a scientific experiment, she was raised in a laboratory in an enormous petri dish in Variable Valley. Since then, Tamara has rarely been seen out of a science lab—or a lab coat!

Lightning antennae brainwaves

Puzzle HQ

Tamara built her own lab at the Observatory at The Port, where she invents new and perplexing brain-teasers for The Puzzle Palace. Tamara is also a keen astronomer and stares at the stars through her Mubble Space Telescope.

Purple hair looks like bolts of electricity.

Ingenious inventor

With her monSTAR problem-solving skills and intelligence, goopendously geeky Tamara busies herself by creating tricky puzzles. She also conducts electrifying (and electrocuting) experiments and investigates fangtastic phenomena!

Clean white starched lab coat

TIAMO

The sweet-natured Sparkly Sweethearts, including the kind and caring Tiamo, are marvellously magical Moshlings who use their shiny, sparkly auras to help out monsters in distress. They can be spotted appearing from out of nowhere in Blisskiss Valley.

Eat your heart out!

Tiamo stays healthy by eating as much fruit as possible. Like all Sparkly Sweethearts, Tiamo avoids gooey food like egg yolks. There's just no room in their diet for anything but fruit!

Tiamo has a magical energy aura.

DATA FILE

Moshling type: Smilies
Species: Sparkly Sweetheart
Habitat: Blisskiss Valley
Smilie sidekick: Rofl

Shiny, healthy appearance—a result of all that fruit and dancing!

Kind-hearted

The Sparkly Sweetheart's warmheartedness means they are the most helpful Moshlings around and are often rushing to someone's rescue. And their sentimental nature influences their music choices too. They love emotional power ballads, and just can't stop d-dumfing to the cheesy beats!

Friendly, welcoming smile

TIDDLES

Somewhat of a local phenomenon in the waters around Monstro City, giant Tiddles actually used to be teeny-weeny! Born as a bit of bait at the end of fisherman George Small's fishing hook, Tiddles escaped his fate as fish food by wriggling into the lake. Chomping on lake-loads of bottom dwelling algae, he soon became 1500 times his former size!

DATA FILE

Hangout: In the water
Catchphrase: "Yodel-ay-eee-ooo!"
Likes: Playing Tiddlesy-winks
Often Spotted: Practicing his singing scales

The voice of a heavenly water creature

No one knows where his tail actually ends...

Fishies play games swimming through Tiddles' "tunnels."

Wet wonder

Talented Tiddles loves to while away his watery days by yodeling to local residents and anyone who wanders his way. He is fast becoming a singing sensation, attracting large crowds with his monstrously beautiful voice.

Sing while you swim

Tuneful Tiddles swims around the lake near Sludge Street. Sometimes he ducks under the water, but he soon pops up again, ready to splash out a new song!

TIKI

The Pilfering Toucan

Tiki and the rest of the cunning gang of Pilfering Toucans nest way up in the highest branches of the tallest trees, close to Lush Lagoon. It's good that they do; these mischievous pirates are wanted in every corner of Monstro City for stealing monstrous amounts of stuff!

Sneaky beakies

Pilfering Toucans will take pretty much anything they can get their beaks on, and that's quite a lot, as their beaks are so big! Hats, salty gobstoppers, Rox... nothing is safe!

Wacky eyes are always on the prize!

Colorful feathers (not useful when hiding!)

Supersized beak for storing plenty of booty

Pilfering playtime

When they're not pilfering, Tiki and this fast-flying throng of pesky pirates enjoy playing the squeeze-box and drinking punch. They also love to lounge on their coconut-hair hammocks while admiring their "finds."

DATA FILE

Moshling type: Birdies
Species: Pilfering Toucan
Habitat: Palm trees near Lush Lagoon
Birdie buddies: DJ Quack, Prof. Purplex, Peppy

193

TINGALING

The kind and generous Kittens of Good Fortune can be spotted catnapping on windowsills and rooftops across Monstro City. Any Moshi who comes across Tingaling or the other fortunate felines is guaranteed good luck, especially if their magic bells are tinkling.

Ghost pirate pet

Poor Tingaling was captured by the ghost pirates of the *Gooey Galleon*, and then blamed when their ship became cursed. Mysteriously, once the crew released their kitty captive, the bad luck curse was lifted!

Cute kittie curl

DATA FILE

Moshling type: Luckies
Species: Kitten of Good Fortune
Habitat: Hong Bong Island
Luckie friends: Penny, O'Really, Furnando

Mystic Moshlings

Kittens of Good Fortune enjoy reading the future in tea leaves and wolfing down fortune cookies. These Luckies are very friendly balls of fluff, but they don't like journalists prying into their kitty-cat business, and they will never ever grant good fortune to those pesky Moshling Puppies!

Magic tinkling bell

One wave of the paw spreads joy and happiness!

TOMBA

The chilly **Wistful Snowtots** live on Mount Sillimanjaro, but sometimes migrate to the Frostipop Glacier to compete in curling championships. Frosty and fragile, poor Snowtots like Tomba are always being kicked apart by abominable creatures, and having their noses nibbled by Funny Bunnies!

Snow alone

The Super Moshis came across poor Tomba's head while on a mission on Mount Sillimanjaro. Thankfully, they soon reunited Tomba's head with its body—and the Snowie was complete again!

Droopy bobble hat

DATA FILE
Moshling type: Snowies
Species: Wistful Snowtot
Habitat: Mount Sillimanjaro
Snowie buddies:
Woolly, Leo, Gracie

Sad Snowtots
Made of ice, snow, and stuff we don't know, Wistful Snowtots are shy, melancholy, and constantly glum. This is probably because they're always struggling to stay cool, listening to sad songs, or being smashed to snowball-sized pieces!

Head loosely fixed to body

Carrot nose often proves too tempting for hungry Bunnies!

195

TRIXIE

You won't catch this fascinating fish floating in Potion Ocean because Trixie prefers to swim in sludgy-green slime streams! Somewhat of a rare breed, she loves feeding on all sorts of strange algae and funny ferns that stick to the banks of the Underground Tunnel slime-ways.

DATA FILE:

Habitat: Slime streams of the Underground Tunnels

Catchphrase:
"I can see a rainbow!"

Likes: Blowing bubbles, changing color

Fin for waving at fans

Fishie on film
Swimming slowly past the doors to The Underground Disco, cute little Trixie often poses for the parades of paparazzi.

Blubbery lips for gobbling algae

Always keeping an extra eye out for rainbows

Rainbow fish

Trixie is able to change her scales to match any color in a rainbow. In fact, you'll often find her hanging out wherever rainbows appear, so she can test out her technicolored transformation talents!

TYRA FANGS

DATA FILE

Hangout: Wherever's hip this week!

Catchphrase: "You are what you wear!"

Likes: Fabulous facials

Fashionista Tyra is a gorgeously glitzy and glamorous Goo Yorker, who now resides in Monstro City. With a sparkling personality and manicured fingernails that are always on the pulse, Tyra was born to be the perfect runway model, TV host, spa owner, and queen of gossip. This is one goopendously talented monster!

Tyra always wears her hair with flair.

A monster can never wear too much bling!

Celebrity couple

When she's not shopping, working, or appearing as a judge at The Underground Disco, Miss Fangs hangs out with her editor boyfriend, Roary Scrawl. Tyra loves telling Roary exactly what to wear, but he never says anything back—Tyra *is* always right, after all!

Rinse and relax!

Need a little pampering? Pop to Tyra's Spa on Ooh La Lane, where she'll cover you with slop, stink, goop, and mud, and you'll come out squeaky clean—promise!

Heels help Tyra strut with style.

WALDO

Tech-savvy Tabby Waldo and the rest of the Nerdicat litter spend their time studying by the grassy knoll on Honeycomb Hill. These clever Moshlings are big Kitties in the wild world of algebra, but they're definitely not wildcats. In fact, they're so dweeby, they actually think that "cool" means a library with air conditioning!

DATA FILE

Moshling type: Kitties

Species: Tabby Nerdicat

Habitat: Honeycomb Hill

Kittie chums: Gingersnap, Purdy, Lady Meowford

He could wear contact lenses, but Waldo loves his thick geeky glasses too much!

Curiosity thrilled the cat!
Inquisitive and inventive Waldo loves tinkering with equipment and experimenting with powerful potions and formulas in his hidden laboratory.

Feline fun

Nerdicats spend their time fixing things and burying their noses in comics. Critters of habit, they listen to the Quantum Physics Hour on Fangdoodle FM every day, while untangling pretzels and munching on toffee nachos. They don't go out much at all, especially not to The Underground Disco, as these masters of math can't dance!

Nerdicats never go anywhere without their calculators.

Having a tail should help with dancing, but Nerdicats trip over theirs.

WALLOP

Crash, bang, Wallop! Raucous Jolly Tubthumpers such as Wallop are extremely loud and energetic, and practice their drumming skills by bashing themselves in the face! They spend most of their time on tour, but are believed to come from the deafening depths of Thwackboom Valley.

Drumtastic dancing
Jolly Tubthumpers like Wallop hate being quiet! They love to drum their own thwacktastic boingy bodies, and can shake, rattle and roll with the best of them!

Drum roll, please!
These thumpin' Tunies love twirling sticks, marching for miles, and drumming on anything and everything that gets in the way! Wallop even played the toadstool drums in Poppets' "I ♥ Moshlings" music video.

DATA FILE
Moshling type: Tunies
Species: Jolly Tubthumper
Habitat: Thwackboom Valley
Tunie teammates: Plinky, Oompah, HipHop

Drumming always puts a big smile on Wallop's face.

Strong arm muscles for powerful drumming!

Feet made for marching

WAVEY DAVEY

Wave hello to Wavey Davey whose favorite way to pass the day is waving to each and every monster in Monstro City! He wore out his best arm, waving like a manic Moshi wave machine, but cheerful chappy Davey ate plenty of wholesome Green, did lots of working out, and is now back to his happy, carefree waving ways.

Stand on me
Davey is best buddies with Underground Tunnel graffiti artist Art Lee. He's always ready to lend a hand, or even head, to his picture-painting pal.

Head full of happy hellos

DATA FILE
Hangout: The Underground Tunnels
Catchphrase: "Hello there!"
Often spotted: Waving away the days

Davey's best waving arm

Well, hello there!
It's not surprising to hear that gesturing gent Davey loves doing the wave, giving high fives, and all kinds of cheery hellos and gracious good-byes. So when you meet him next, be sure to give him a wave or two!

WEEVIL KNEEVIL

Weevil Kneevil weaves and winds his way through the crowds on Main Street, delivering packages between Yukea and Bizarre Bazaar. There is a rumor racing around that he's actually delivering love letters between the shopkeepers, but Weevil insists this isn't true.

DATA FILE

Hangout: Main Street
Catchphrase: "Wheelie wild wheelies"
Likes: Stunts, mountain biking down Mount Sillimanjaro

Ears flap in the wind as Weevil flies around.

Hard helmet for hazardous falls

Tour de Monstro City

Speedy Weevil loves tearing around the streets of Monstro City and is very attached to his shiny orange bike. In fact, you'll rarely see him not on it, except when he falls off it, that is!

Accidents happen

Weevil has been known to have the occasional biking mishap, but he accepts that they're simply part of the winding path that is his crazy courier career!

Tough tires for stunt biking

WHITE FANG

White Fang and the other Musky Huskies don't stay in one place for very long, though it's not uncommon to spot their scruffy tails poking out of a trash can as they look for leftovers. That's because these ravenous and ferociously food-focused hobo hounds will do pretty much anything for their doggy dinners!

Yummy fingers!
Monsters must be careful when they give White Fang a bone. He's so ravenous that he might just bite their fingers by mistake! What a dog-astrophy that would be!

A dog's dinner!
Hungry Muskies are so busy searching for doggy chow, they often neglect simple hygiene rules. The mucky pups hate de-tangling lotion, so their fur is constantly messy. And their stench suggests they're not big fans of soap either!

Fur in need of a pooch parlor visit!

Mucky face from guzzling garbage

DATA FILE
Moshling type: Puppies
Species: Musky Husky
Habitat: Various dumpsters
Puppie pals: Fifi, McNulty, Scamp

Nose can detect garbage a mile away.

WING, FANG, SCREECH, AND SONAR

Wing, Fang, Screech, and Sonar are batty bat siblings who terrified the monsters of Monstro City so much, they were banished from Ecto's Cave! These frightening flying mammals now like to hang out (upside down) in The Underground Tunnels.

Snoozing on the ceiling!

Going underground

If you wander deep into the damp Underground Tunnels, you could be in for a webbed-winged surprise. These flying four could flap right into your face! Well, it *is* dark down there!

Fangs look scary but are actually harmless.

Big bat ears for hearing personal conversations

Bat chat!

These scarily chatty batties are always keeping their eyes and pointy ears out for gossip, which they then tattle to *The Daily Growl*. Hidden in the dingy tunnels, they're perfectly positioned to overhear monstrously scandalous conversations and whispers!

DATA FILE
Hangout: The Underground Tunnels
Catchphrase: "Have you heard..."
Likes: Chitchatting, telling tales
Often spotted: Hanging around

WOOLLY

Titchy-Tusked Mammoths like Woolly can be found snoozing and snoring in the ChillyBot State Park or chomping hoodle plants in the Unknown Zone on Music Island. These snuffly Snowies are simple, old-fashioned creatures who love blow-drying their fabulously fluffy blue hair and eating even fluffier cotton candy kebabs!

Titchy-Tusked Mammoths are very shy, so they hide behind their fluffy fur!

DATA FILE

Moshling type: Snowies
Species: Titchy-Tusked Mammoth
Habitat: ChillyBot State Park or the Unknown Zone on Music Island
Snowie buddies: Tomba, Leo, Gracie

Bewildered beast

Nobody knew the Titchy-Tusked Mammoths even existed until the Super Moshis and Woolly Blue Hoodoos discovered them deep in the Gombala Gombala jungle. Poor Woolly was left feeling a bit dazed after this rude awakening!

Shaggy chic

Mammoth Moshlings like spending their time dyeing their fur blue with Inka Inka essence and putting their ears and feet in gloopy green puddles to perfect their look. They never cut or style their fur, and if they get too hot, they just take it all off—like a woolly coat!

Big nostrils for sniffing!

Teeny tusks are sharpened using chalk.

WURLEY

The Twirly Tiddlycopter

DATA FILE
Moshling type: Techies
Species: Twirly Tiddlycopter
Habitat: Anywhere high in the sky
Techie teammates: Holga, Gabby, Nipper

Flocks of noisy Tiddlycopters, including the twirly Wurley, zoom around the Moshi world, carrying Rox and other valuables. They hum classical music as they fly, and when not on important missions, they enjoy looping in circles over Hangar Eight-and-a-Half, or taking in the sights high above Nuttanbolt Lake.

Mighty flighty Moshlings
These cheery choppers chomp on delicious wind socks dipped in oil and love days when there's not a cloud in the sky! They don't like rain, because it rusts the nuts and bolts on their tin flying jackets. But most of all these Techies don't like nasty Dr. Strangeglove, especially since he used their spinning propellers to power his evil glumping machine!

Super fast rotary headgear

Bluey-green paint job means Wurley blends into the sky.

Aerial workout
Listen out for the wokka-wokka sound as the Tiddlycopters fly overhead! Daring Wurley loves whirling through the clouds and performing rotar-raising sky stunts including loop-the-loops and Wurley-gig whooshes.

Specially designed tin flying jacket

ZACK BINSPIN

Baby Zack first dreamed about becoming a famous singer while watching Screech McPiehole yelling on TV show "Top of the Mops." Little did Zack know that Simon Growl would soon discover him singing in his garbage bin in Brashcan Alley, and save him from impending garbage-dump doom! And now Moptop Tweenybop Binspin is a sensational gooperstar!

DATA FILE

Moshling type: RoxStar
Species: Moptop Tweenybop
Habitat: Brashcan Alley and Sandy Drain Hotel
Celebrity pal: Bobbi SingSong

Binspin Mania

Simon Growl's HighPants Productions filmed the music video for Zack's song, "Moptop Tweenybop (My Hair's Too Long)" in Brashcan Alley. The goopendous video launched Monstro City's Binspin Mania!

Celebrity Mop-star

When he's not on tour, cute but conceited Zack spends most of his time at the Sandy Drain Hotel, where he likes washing, conditioning, gooing, and combing his fashionable hair. He also loves shouting, "Check out my lid!" to everyone he meets.

Big hair covering a big head!

Pitch-perfect pop voice

ZACK

Vain Zack loves to wear a t-shirt with his own name printed on it.

ZOMMER

Zommers are freaky, mixed-up monsters who think it's cool to drool and unravel themselves! They're not sure why it is that they keep coming apart at the edges, but it probably has something to do with the fact that they love picking at their seams and stitches!

Teeny tiny Zommers

Baby Zommers aren't the cutest of mini Moshi Monsters—they scream, drool, and barf more than any Moshi! Most monsters grow out of such habits, but fully grown Zommers are just as dribbly!

Spikey rotten rock MonSTAR's hair!

Big mouth for extra dribble power

DATA FILE

Hangout: Monstro City

Catchphrases: "Need a hand!", "Drool lickin' fun!"

Monster mates: Diavlo, Furi, Katsuma, Luvli, Poppet

Feelin' totally Zommerific, dude!

Rock 'n' unravel

These salivating, eye-poppin' one-eyed eyesores think that playing the guitar is utterly awesome. A rotting group of the messy, musical Zommers recorded the track "Rock Like A Zommer" on the Music Rox album, and it was a huge Moshi hit!

207

LONDON, NEW YORK, MELBOURNE, MUNICH, AND DELHI

US Assistant Managing Editor: Allison Singer
US Editorial Director: Nancy Ellwood
Senior Editor: Helen Murray
Editorial Assistant: Ruth Amos
Additional Editors: Elizabeth Dowsett,
David Fentiman, Emma Grange
Senior Designer: Lynne Moulding
Designer: Thelma-Jane Robb
Additional Designers: Rachel Bush, Liam Drane,
Guy Harvey, Satvir Sihota, Rhys Thomas
Managing Editor: Laura Gilbert
Design Manager: Maxine Pedliham
Art Director: Ron Stobbart
Publisher: Simon Beecroft
Publishing Director: Alex Allan
Pre-Production Producer: Siu Chan
Senior Producer: Shabana Shakir

First published in the United States in 2013
by DK Publishing
375 Hudson Street, New York, New York 10014

10 9 8 7 6 5 4 3 2 1
001–187414–Feb/2013

Published in Great Britain by Dorling Kindersley Limited.

A catalog record for this book is available from the Library of Congress.

ISBN: 978-1-4654-0186-1

Color reproduction by Altaimage Ltd, UK
Printed and bound by South China Printing Co Ltd, China

ACKNOWLEDGMENTS
Dorling Kindersley would like to thank:
Rahul Ganguly for proofreading; Jack McCall at Mind Candy;
and Samantha Mitchell and James Wing at Vivid.

Discover more at
www.dk.com
www.moshimonsters.com